First published in Great Britain in 1999 by VISION
Paperbacks, a division of Satin Publications Limited.

VISION Paperbacks,
a division of
Satin Publications Limited
20 Queen Anne Street
London W1M 0AY
Email: sheenadewan@compuserve.com

Layout: Justine Hounam
Printed and bound by The Bath Press Ltd.

©1999 Andrew Gauntlett
ISBN: 1-901250-25-3

Net Spies

Who's Watching You on the Web?

Andrew Gauntlett

Edited by Sheena Dewan

Acknowledgements

Writing this, my first book, has for numerous reasons proved to be a task more arduous than I first imagined. Many, many people have helped, advised, and encouraged (sometimes without them knowing it!). It is to them I express my gratitude. Mentors to whom I am grateful are Dr Kit Lester, Bernard Sufrin, Dennis Woods, Dr Stephen Jarvis, Sam Hey, Dr David Acheson, and Professor Tony Hoare. I am also most grateful, and somewhat apologetic, to the friends and confidantes whom I have neglected during this difficult period. Those I would most like to thank, for the reasons mentioned above, are (in no particular order): Professor Ian Holmes, Dr Joseph Edward Nemec, Dr Arnold Koopman, Dr Eric Oden Morehead, Dr Martin Kjellstrand, Mr Ian Miller, Steven and Atsuko Brown, Ken Ehrett, Tim Fitzmaurice (and Sarah!), Eisen Chao, Dan Browne, Jolene Franks, Filip Camerman, Marc and Annalise van Dikkenberg, Ijdo Dijkstra, Ingo Mittendorf, TJ Miller, Tom Beam, Douglas Shultz, Brian Pickrell, Tobias Reker (where's my blade, Tobi?), Douglas Shultz, Henrik Jonssn, Morten Geday, Phil Young, Daniel Smilov, Alex "Girl's Name" Shirley, and John Gerald Birkenshaw. Lastly this would be incomplete without my expression of a special thank you to Bulgarian chess master Boyan Tonkov whose encouragement and enthusiasm originally inspired this work. To anyone that I have forgotten, and to those who have asked not to be mentioned, I also express my sincerest gratitude.

About the Author

Andrew Gauntlett has many years experience in computer communications, both as a user and as a programmer. His dissertation for his BSc in Computer Science at Portsmouth University was on the Legal Issues of Privacy and Encryption. In 1998 he completed a Master's Degree in Computation at the University of Oxford (Jesus College), where he specialised in formal software design and wrote a thesis on intelligent communications protocols. At present, Andrew is working as a consultant to the investment banking sector within the City of London, and also as a freelance journalist reporting on the social and legal aspects of computing. Net Spies is Andrew's first book.

The author may be contacted via the publisher, or by email at author@net-spies.co.uk
ThePGP public key is available at:
http://www.net-spies.co.uk/public.key

Contents

x

Dedicated to...

-----BEGIN PGP MESSAGE-----

qANQR1DDBAQDAAHJf+yCNCOW9YoWz8cPFYA16rkQ9upCbd3zzhk17OjH5f2KNPjl
WE40Di3x8KQVsFHLaU1oNMO8scVX5uu9w+sDHX+A+LmTfeEoo73tsoG4GNy6izhf
UOrAWXddvTDcW6GT5ZnFfh1mEL9UoGBK+Xl5AiKQ4oAPyqrb4g76Io7kt/Q=
=40Up

-----END PGP MESSAGE-----

Think, in your head, *now*, think of the most...
private... secret... intimate thing you have ever
done secure in the knowledge of its privacy... Are
you thinking of it? ... *Well, I saw you do it!*

Tom Stoppard (1937 -)
Rosencrantz and Guildenstern Are Dead (1967)

privacy n.

1a the state of being private and undisturbed.
b a person's right to this.
2 freedom from intrusion or public attention.
3 avoidance of publicity

(Oxford English Dictionary)

INTRODUCTION

Do you believe you have a private life? If so, you may need to think again. Cast your mind back over the events of today, or indeed any average day; do you have a credit card? A mobile phone perhaps? Do you ever drive your car into town? Maybe on your way to buy this book, you walked through the town centre, past a number of CCTV cameras. While you were browsing the shelves in your local bookstore, you were probably being watched by in-store security cameras. Perhaps you paid for this book by credit card.

If you did any one of the above things, then your name, and your 'numbers' have already come to the attention of possibly hundreds of computers around the world.

This is the side of the information age that they don't want you to know about. After all, information is power, and power is money and those that hold the information are holding a valuable commodity; the ability to trade in pure information. The market for data is one of the fastest growing sectors of the market. The information technology (IT) industry consistently outperforms all other sectors, its development driven by the insatiable need of both corporations and governments to gain ever more information on us – the public. Companies are driven by their shareholders desire for higher dividends, as well as their own hunger for a greater market share. Their aim is to build profiles on consumers so they can manipulate their tastes. Governments, on the other hand, seek to control their population through mass surveillance.

I believe that citizens of any culture have the right to privacy as well as the freedom to express themselves, the freedom of association and the freedom of access to information. In many countries, these rights are enshrined in a constitution, or law, and even if not, they are supposedly guaranteed. The media tells us on an almost daily basis, however, that those rights are being abused on the

Internet by pornographers, paedophiles and fraudsters. There is clearly the potential for conflict on a grand scale between the right to privacy and the right to freedom of speech.

One might ask why we should specifically care about privacy on the Internet when so many areas of our lives are becoming subject to scrutiny on a daily basis by governments and companies alike. Thinking about security on the Internet is essential because of the global nature of the World Wide Web. As its very name suggests, it transcends all national boundaries; it is the true 'global village'. Sitting at a computer, you could access a web page that was put together by someone in the next street or on the other side of the world – and you would not necessarily be able to tell the difference. You could research anything – or be researched, and there are, depending on where you are in the world, very few laws to limit you – or protect you. And, even if there were, one could argue that due to the international nature of the Internet, there would be very little that could be done to enforce those laws or seek redress.

In many respects, the Internet is ungoverned – it is not subject to international laws, even though it is an international phenomenon; it is easily accessible and it cannot viably be policed.

The Internet gives individuals the ability to say and do what they want online, especially when technology is coupled with anonymity. Issues of copyright, libel, obscenity all fly out of the window – anything goes. Many people feel that this anonymity is essential to guarantee free speech, especially in cases where people are in fear of the authorities reactions to what they have to say. Campaigners for democracy living in oppressive regimes, such as Burma and Tibet, have used the Internet to bring their causes to the attention of the West. This is no doubt a right that must be defended, but we cannot get away from the fact that it is a provision that can – and is – abused. The media is quick to tell us that child pornographers can use the Internet to easily share their disgusting material. Private financial information is published on the Web. Hidden cameras can broadcast our private moments in the toilet or changing room to a paying audience.

These are examples of absolute free speech that are entered into with freedom from responsibility. So how can the absolute right to freedom of speech be reconciled with the fundamental right to privacy, as enshrined in the UN Convention of Human Rights? To many people, the ideas of freedom of speech and privacy are mutually exclusive, and when given a choice, majority opinion seems to fall in favour of freedom of speech. But can this really be the case? Is it reasonable for freedom of speech to extend to someone using that right to publish unlisted telephone numbers? One would think that an unlisted number – a service provided by most telephone companies, is a service geared towards privacy. And yet, this has frequently happened on the Internet.

This age-old dilemma looks set to explode on the international stage at any time, as North America and Western Europe have completely opposing stances on this matter. The United States has constitutional laws regarding freedom of speech but will not update privacy laws for the Internet. Europe's situation is the reverse. This is very important given that the future of commerce is increasingly coming to mean online trade, and neither side seems willing to back down. The potential for European-North American trade online is enormous, and one of the commodities is pure information, which the US wants to profit from, and Europe wishes to protect.

Most of the books currently available on Internet privacy tend to focus on how to use particular software packages, which complement the often unread – or even unreadable – user manual. Others are aimed more at how to exploit the lack of privacy on the Net. I hope that there will be those in the IT industry reading this book with an interest in the ethics of their industry – for it is programmers that create the systems that are used by the public to 'surf the Net'. Given that there is an absence of a professional body with regulatory powers in the IT industry, it is up to each individual to formulate their own code of ethics.

System administrators have access to all their users' personal details, and can even read personal emails if they so choose. The vast majority of system administrators have a strong, albeit unspoken code of ethics that they adhere to, which prevents them from abusing this power. In the absence of regulations, which I believe we must have, it is up to IT professionals, corporations and governments alike to formulate their own code of ethics. There are a growing number of professionals in the IT industry, including those at the pinnacle of their career who are moving into the realm of politics, and perhaps the leading example is Mitch Kapor. He has many achievements under his belt; he designed the best-selling spreadsheet Lotus 1-2-3 and was the founder of the massive Lotus Corporation. But in June 1990, he left the industry to co-found the Electronic Frontier Foundation – which in their words is, 'a non-profit civil liberties organisation working in the public interest to protect privacy, free expression, and access to public resources and information online, as well as to promote responsibility in new media'.

But it is also up to the public to ensure that they are adequately protected, and it is simply not good enough to believe that it is not the problem of the individual. Because, even if you never use the Internet, your personal details are out there in some form, and those details can be accessed by the public. Now that more of our information is being stored on computer than ever before, and that computers are being linked together, we are facing the insidious trend towards an almost total recording of a person's actions throughout their lives, as George Orwell warned would happen. This might even one day extend to the recording and storing of telephone conversations for life. Something you say on the telephone now could be held up to you in ten years time by a prospective employer, and it could prevent you from getting the job. Do you think this is far-fetched? Employers regularly scan Internet message boards, looking for postings from the people applying for a job. Most of these messages are considered as private conversations, which should never be related to a person's professional activities.

Net Spies assumes no knowledge or understanding of computers, but I hope that it will be of interest to both the public and the industry alike. Personal privacy is being abused as we speak on the Internet, by malicious individuals, corporations and governments – it is a contemporary and pressing issue that affects us all.

Net Spies

PRIVACY MATTERS

The World Wide Web ('The Web') has transformed global communications. An exciting new service, it provides the user with seemingly limitless access to news, products and services. The Web is an entirely new medium for entertainment, communication and self-expression.

The world is ringed by a telephone system that connects every city in every country. When a computer is plugged into the phone system it can access multimedia information via the Internet, which is delivered on demand to the home or office. With a single phone call, it is possible to connect, reconnect and jump between an almost immeasurable number of online services. Unlike previous methods of delivering information, such as television, the Web is not a one-way broadcast medium. Rather, it allows two-way access like the telephone. Internet users can send and receive email, participate in real-time chat, and produce their own information services (web sites) for others to access at leisure. More advanced services include the ability to send faxes straight off the computer screen, telephone calls, and even participation in video conferencing at much cheaper rates than currently offered by telephone companies.

The Web was originally designed by a student in Geneva and it was intended to be a system that would deliver experimental data to scientists, but its flexibility, power and potential has ensured its spread into a much larger market place. The Web was only introduced to the public in the early 1990s and yet the growth in demand for web-based services has been phenomenal; the growth in numbers of people accessing the Web far surpasses the take-up rate of any previous new technology.

It is predicted that by the early years of the new millennium, use of the Web will be at least as widespread as the telephone or TV today. Indeed, many industry experts believe that the Internet will take over from the telephone as the dominant communications medium in the 21st century. Mail order companies are virtually salivating over the money-spinning potential of the Web, while credit organisations are busying themselves in the quest to produce electronic cash in a form suitable for this lucrative emerging global marketplace.

The Web is set to change society as fundamentally and irrevocably as did television, the telephone and the printing press. And, the impact will be all the more profound because the Web has the capacity to incorporate all prior communications technologies.

The rapid expansion of the Web has been made possible by its simple design as well as its ability to exploit existing technologies and infrastructure, such as public telephone networks and the private telephony networks owned by multinational conglomerates. From its inception, governments, companies and individuals alike have rushed to obtain a presence on the Web with little thought as to the potential risks involved. Using the Web, it is possible for anyone who knows where to look to retrieve large quantities of information about individuals that was once considered personal and private. Medical records, home addresses, credit details, unlisted telephone numbers – the list is almost endless. All of these and more have found their way onto the Web, usually without the individual's knowledge or consent. This is a problem that affects everyone and not just those who use the Web, although for Web users themselves, the problem of maintaining privacy is, if anything, even larger. Everything a person does is recorded, logged and analysed. There is a veritable 'information gold rush' in progress, as government departments and commercial organisations strive to become 'information rich' through the acquisition of massive databases on the habits and activities, likes and dislikes of individuals. This information is often gathered from Web users without their even being aware that it is happening, or their knowing for what purpose the information will be used. And, as if this were not bad enough, much of the information stored on individuals is inaccurate. The methods used to collect information about individuals can be unscrupulous.

In 'Privacy Online', a June 1998 report by the Federal Trade Commission to the US Congress, there was mention of one web site aimed at children, specifically geared to persuading them to provide information on their parents' private and personal financial information. The web site included questions such as: have they ever received a gift [from their parents] in the form of stocks, savings bonds, mutual funds or certificates of deposits? Have they ever invested cash gifts in mutual funds, stocks or bonds? Do their parents own any mutual funds etc.? The web site neglected to warn the children that they should ask their parents for permission before providing such financial details. Neither did the site, according to the report, appear to take any steps to involve the parents, nor give any information as to how the information would be used. It is highly likely that such data would be sold on, which is legal in the US, but against the law in the EU. However, due to the international nature of the Internet, it is possible for children in Europe to find this site and fill in the form, unwittingly being used as a source of information gathered and distributed illegally.

Governments are also seizing the opportunities of the Web, and other forms of electronic communication, to substantially increase their routine surveillance of the general population. The technology that enables all the benefits of the Web can also used to spy upon, and monitor people with little more than a flick of a switch. Data gathered from the Web can be analysed automatically by dedicated spy computers. As this book will show, the monitoring and analysis of email is carried out by security agents on a routine and widespread basis. Mass surveillance is the stuff of dystopian novels such as Orwell's '1984' and is often flippantly dismissed.

However, there are a growing number of voices worldwide that are claiming that Big Brother is alive and well and living in cyberspace, watching and recording your every move.

As Simon Davies, Director General of Privacy International and visiting fellow at the London School of Economics, writes: 'A Global Information Infrastructure – potentially the greatest force since the birth of the automobile – is being forged. Mass surveillance is developing from Argentina to Zambia not merely through video cameras, DNA profiling, satellite surveillance, police systems and credit reporting agencies, but through a vast range of computer-based surveillance mechanisms.

'Even now, mobile phones and bank machines create a real-time geographical tracking mechanism. Search engines on the Internet present a detailed picture of people's activities and interests. Data matching allows authorities to link computers from different areas of the public and private sector. The advent of this surveillance society will bring with it a new era of social control.'

The Web is the public face of the global information infrastructure that Davies speaks of. Civil liberties groups, worried by the threat to personal privacy and lack of democratic accountability, are demanding proper legal safeguards to be established.

Business organisations, eager to exploit the lucrative opportunities of online trade are, for once, siding with the civil liberties groups in these demands. Governments, however, are attempting to outlaw the very technology that both the public and businesses are demanding. The technology of privacy is the technology of encryption, which until recently, governments around the world have kept a firm hold upon.

Encryption is the technical term for the well-known method of 'scrambling' text or conversations; written messages have been encrypted by leaders and schoolboys alike for centuries, and so many Hollywood spy movies have shown the use of telephonic scramblers. But it is not merely a fiction; advanced telephone scrambling devices were used – and still are used – for diplomatic phone calls, such as the infamous 'Hotline' between Washington and Moscow during the Cold War.

The uses and necessity of encryption in modern communications can be illustrated by having a look at another recently developed communications medium; the cellular telephone network. When mobile phones were first introduced in the 1980s, anyone with an all-band radio receiver could intercept and monitor cellular telephone calls.

This worrying fact made headline news around the world in 1990, when transcripts of a private conversation between Diana, Princess of Wales and one of her lovers, James Gilbey became widely available. The conversation had been allegedly recorded independently by two eavesdroppers using inexpensive radio equipment. If one telephone conversation was actually recorded by two people, one can only imagine the extent of the surveillance by radio enthusiasts and others in that period.

This was not the only security problem with early mobile phones. If the radio receiver that was monitoring such phones was connected to a personal computer, it was possible to obtain the telephone number and matching serial number of the mobile phones. For example, hackers have been breaking into the telephone system since the Sixties – although they were then known as

'Phone Phreakers'. Hacking (or indeed phone phreaking) are still common activities on the Internet, and hackers even get together periodically at organised conferences. On the way to one of these conferences held at Manchester, England, one hacker had a laptop computer and a mobile phone on the train with her. She was able to access the telephone network and obtain the number of every other telephone on that train. As a mocking demonstration of her hacking prowess she made every telephone ring simultaneously – much to the chagrin of the self appointed 'cellular experts' on board.

The telephone and identification numbers of early mobile phones were easy to intercept. With this information, a thief could 'clone' the electronic information belonging specifically to the mobile telephone, transfer it onto a new phone and sell it as a phone that could make free phone calls. But the phone calls were not really free; the calls would actually appear on the bill of the person who legitimately owned that number.

The threat of eavesdropping and identity theft associated with early mobile phones led to a loss in confidence and, consequently, to a loss of customers and revenue for mobile phone companies. These problems were only resolved with the introduction of digital mobile phones, which encrypt all the private information, such as the telephone number, the SIM card number and the conversation itself.

Governments initially resisted the introduction of encryption on mobile phones, on the basis that they might need to legitimately 'tap' the calls of suspect individuals, who might be engaging in illegal activities. However, a compromise was reached with the advent of digital mobile phones; calls are now encrypted using a method which can be unscrambled by certain government departments and police employees.

Many, including civil liberties organisations, oppose the introduction of such a scheme for the Web. One of the most highly visible online is the 'Blue Ribbon' in support of the Electronic Frontier Foundation's (EFF) campaign for free speech online. The EFF is a civil liberties pressure group that provides support and resources to protect the rights of Web users. It promotes privacy, freedom of expression, and the right to use the Web without fear. Parallels can be drawn between the mobile communications network and the Web. Quite rightly, it is perceived as being insecure, and encryption is regarded by many as the way forward. Study after study by banks, market research companies and legislative bodies have shown that the lack of privacy is the biggest single factor dissuading people from conducting trade on the Web. Conclusions consistently show that the use of encryption would help to allay public fears about doing business and sending personal mail over the Web. A confidential internal report by a major high street bank says that whereas over 70 per cent of its customers trust a 'hole-in-the-wall' cash machine only 5 per cent would send out their credit card details over an unencrypted Web.

This time in the case of the Web, the use of encryption is meeting with much stronger resistance from governments than it did with mobile phones. The difference between scrambling phone calls and data sent over the Web is that the computer user is completely in control of the method of encryption that they use, and can therefore use codes of any strength they desire. This means it could be virtually impossible for anyone other than the intended recipient to intercept and decode. The argument goes that this could compromise governments' obligations to maintain law and order, on the grounds that they would be unable to monitor illegal and subversive activities online.

Net Spies

So why does the Web user need encryption and just what are the threats that the average computer user faces? The Internet knows no international boundaries and criminal hackers can target victims abroad. It is not difficult to eavesdrop on email or gain access to personal files stored on the hard disk of a computer hooked up to a phone line. If a personal file contains information such as a credit card number, quick and easy profits can be fraudulently amassed. In the case of hackers operating internationally, they are working across national borders, and so detection, capture and trial is a costly and time-consuming process requiring international co-operation. Additionally, because the Web handles digital data in a 'machine readable' form, it is very easy for governments and other large organisations to monitor the public's activities on the Web on a wide scale basis.

Surveillance of individuals used to be a very laborious process, involving the tapping of telephones or tailing a suspect with anything up to six agents following a person. Although conventional methods are still used, nowadays it is relatively easy to pinpoint people's activities; a single desktop computer has the capacity to monitor the email of tens of thousands of people simultaneously. This electronic spy – or network of electronic spy machines – never sleeps, never misses a single move, and dutifully reports any activity it has been programmed to regard as suspicious to its masters, as we will see in chapter three.

If this sounds far-fetched, consider the following example. Two men, William Newell, aged 59, and Wendal Hazelton, aged 40, were arrested by a high-tech-crimes police unit in Silicon Valley and charged with duping companies out of hundreds of thousands of dollars. From their trailer home in California they set up web sites of non-existent companies and used these sites to gain fraudulent loans. The pair had also been copying the Web pages of legitimate companies and using them to forge letterheads and purchase orders. The pair had even used the Web to research potential victims. Sgt. Don Brister, in charge of the Police Department's high-tech-crime unit said, 'This is more elaborate a fraud scheme than normally we run across'.

Even though the technology exists to protect people from foul play on the Web, they are still at risk. This book will describe those risks and will argue that governments are aware of the dangers, but are not taking steps to protect their citizens from Internet fraud because the existing loopholes allow them to routinely spy on their nation's communications. Not only is the lack of safeguards allowing governmental surveillance, but it also allows unscrupulous marketeers to dossier and manipulate data on the activities, tastes and preferences of consumers, which facilitates aggressive and intrusive sales techniques, such as 'spam', and the flouting of international laws on obscenity, fraud, and copyright.

Central to this entangled problem is the notion of personal privacy, and it is worth taking the time to examine just what privacy is, and how the law protects the right to it.

The right to privacy is recognised as fundamental in the United Nations Declaration of Human Rights. A fundamental right is one that may, under certain circumstances, be waived, as opposed to an absolute right, which is inviolable. Privacy can be loosely separated into broad categories; bodily, territorial, communications, and data.

Bodily privacy is the right not to have one's person interfered with by procedures such as invasive body searches and drug testing. In the UK, such procedures may only be carried out by authorised persons and then only when law enforcement officials demonstrate reasonable grounds for suspicion. Recently however, the governing body of medical practitioners in the UK, the General Medical Council, advised doctors against performing cavity searches on suspects since they may be risking legal action on the grounds of abuse.

Territorial privacy is the essence of the oft-heard saying that 'an Englishman's home is his castle'. People are entitled to have a private space of their own and this right is generally granted. In most western countries, people have a right to privacy in their own homes, a right that extends to the use of reasonable force to defend their home against intruders.

Kenneth Noye, Britain's most wanted man, used this right to his advantage when he stabbed and killed a police officer who was investigating his home without a warrant. Noye was cleared of murder charges when the court agreed that he was defending his home from what he thought was an intruder.

Communications privacy is the right to conduct conversations in private. For example, lawyer-client and doctor-patient conversations are protected in law as absolute. It could be argued that in reality, the right to communications privacy can only be fundamental. If the right to communicate in private were absolute, then investigative resources such as phone taps, mail interception, and other forms of eavesdropping, including web surveillance, would not be allowed on the grounds of privacy invasion. The right to private communications is protected inasmuch as a court order is necessary for wiretapping – although the law and practice differs widely between Europe and the US. Email, faxes, and telephone calls are routinely monitored on a mass basis and court orders are only sought when the material thus gained is to be cited as evidence. Recent moves by the UK government are providing for such court permission to be granted retrospectively.

Data privacy is a modern concept made necessary by the proliferation of computer systems. Enormous quantities of data is held on individuals in the West and systems which hold this information are networked. Increasingly computer databases are sharing sensitive information, which leads to the new threat of 'dataveillance', whereby those with access to the necessary computer systems or networks can build up detailed and intimate profiles on target individuals.

Dataveillance is defined by Roger Clarke, Visiting Fellow at the Department of Computer Science of the Australian National University as 'the systematic use of personal data systems in the investigation or monitoring of the actions or communications of one or more persons'. For example, the whereabouts of a person carrying a mobile telephone can be pinpointed with considerable accuracy whenever the phone is switched on. One can imagine a computer system that holds a database of all the active mobile telephones in a country and systematically tracks the location of those phones, storing the information in another database. The nature of the cellular network makes this an inexpensive process that would provide investigative officials with an almost complete record of the mobile phone owning nation's movements.

The European Convention on Human Rights also establishes a fundamental right to privacy. Article Eight of the convention asserts that: '1. Everyone has the right to respect for his private and family life, his home and his correspondence. 2. There shall be no interference by a public authority with the exercise of this right except such as is in accordance with the law and is necessary in a democratic society in the interests of national security, public safety or the economic well-being of the country, for the prevention of disorder or crime, for the protection of health or morals, or for the protection of the rights and freedoms of others'.

The second Article is a bone of contention for users of the Web. The freely available encryption technology that the Web has to offer makes it impossible for anyone, government or otherwise, to interfere with correspondence and this could hinder the attempts of public authorities to fulfil their duty to protect. Because the Web is a worldwide public network, it is practically impossible to prevent the spread of this technology. This was never a problem with privately operated communications networks where governments usually license operators and insist that licensees only use equipment that is 'tappable'. Often governments have funded this aspect of the technology by giving grants to private network operators to install the necessary surveillance devices or modify the equipment accordingly. The Digital Telephony Act in the United States requires all telephone operators to use only 'tappable' equipment. The Web has all but invalidated this law since communications on the Web can be made untappable by anybody. If secrecy is desired, then freely available 'scrambling' technology can be run on an ordinary PC.

The cellular phone network, like the credit card verification networks, is a privately operated network and largely trusted by consumers. On the whole, people recognise that the government has a duty to maintain law and order and in order to protect the public it is understood that the authorities may need to access privately owned records if it assists in capturing criminals.

Accountability is supposedly ensured as these records may only be accessed by court order. The Web differs radically from cellular phones and credit card verification in that it is a public network. Anyone with access to the Web can offer services for any purpose, with only one restriction: that they are not breaking the laws of the country they are located in. So, for example, in countries where hard core pornography is legal, many profitable web sites have appeared to distribute material to countries where it is still illegal. And those running these web sites are not breaking the law.

Personal privacy on public data is an issue that concerns the majority of the population, and not just those who actively use those networks. In the last two decades, an increasing amount of personal information is being stored on more and more computer systems, and the average citizen of developed nations is recorded on more files and in greater detail than ever before in history. According to UK's Channel 4 documentary series, Equinox, the amount of personal information is staggering; European and US citizens are recorded on up to 200 different computers, and on any given day of the year, their names will pass between seven and twenty computer systems. Almost every detail of a person's economic life history is now recorded somewhere, as a result of the adoption of the so-called 'cash-less society'. Employment histories, family details, criminal records, credit histories, and in some countries, even medical records are routinely stored on computers.

One of the earliest commercial applications of office computers was as a replacement for the filing cabinet. Indeed, data stored on computer is still referred to as a file, with groups of related files being kept in folders. It was a natural progression for organisations to transfer information already possessed on paper to computers. As computers became more commonplace, firms developed more ways to analyse, exploit and ideally profit from their stored information. The 'data imperative' was born, as corporations and government departments discovered that information itself had become a commodity.

Net Spies

Both the public and private sectors desired the acquisition of data so that they could improve their efficiency and facilitate decision making. In those early days – during the 1960s – the US government debated the notion of setting up a National Data Center to support socioeconomic research. This met with fierce resistance, most notably from Representative Frank Horton, who astutely observed that 'one of the most practical of our present safeguards of privacy is the fragmented nature of present information. It is scattered in little bits and pieces across the geography and years of our life. Retrieval is impractical and often impossible. A central data bank removes completely this safeguard.'

Until recently, the massive amount of data stored on individuals on various private and public networks has been kept separate, and this dispersal of data has afforded some protection of privacy. With the advent of the Internet and the Web these networks have been brought together. Modern database management systems are able to seamlessly access many of these widely dispersed databases making the entire Web appear as one huge, central databank. Protection of data by dispersal is no longer an adequate safeguard. Take, for example, the unnerving tale of retired Hollywood songwriter Foreman Brown who was incorrectly pronounced dead by his bank's computer.

Brown first became aware that there was a problem when his cheques were returned marked 'deceased'. Next, his welfare payments were stopped. Perhaps mildly alarmed, but generally unperturbed at being given the unexpected news of his own demise, Brown set off for the Social Security offices to have the error rectified. This was easier said than done: the administrators gave him short shrift, assuring him that such a mistake could never happen, and if the computer said he was dead, then dead he must be. Ever the optimist, Brown decided that his living presence there in the welfare office must surely convince somebody in authority that he was not dead. He decided to give the matter a little time, and spend the night watching a movie. In the video rental store, his American Express credit card was rejected. The young counter assistant tore up his card in front of his very eyes, not to mention the gleeful eyes of the other customers in the store.

Apparently, the Amex credit verification system had also heard of Brown's death and was not taking any chances.

Unfortunately for Brown, one of the supposed benefits of storing information on computer is that computers are able to communicate faster than humans. Whilst Brown was attempting to convince the sceptical staff at the welfare centre that he was alive, the digital rumours of his death were spreading from one computer to another. It was as if the networked computer systems were aware of their error and trying their own methods to rectify it, and his medicare payments were stopped. It took Foreman Brown a whole year to sort out the error and rebuild his life, which he clung onto, despite repeated computerised and administrative assurances to the contrary.

The above example illustrates how computer systems owned by both the public and private sectors are sharing our personal information. Brown's problem arose because his data became polluted with false information. Doubtless it all started because an overworked data entry clerk made a simple error when typing in a form, but this problem brought untold distress and took a whole year to rectify. One solution being forwarded to prevent this kind of error reoccurring is that databases should identify people from a single, and unified reference number.

A social security number (SSN), or a personal telephone number could, for example, be issued at birth so that it remains associated with the person for life. This suggestion horrifies many privacy campaigners, as it would actually make dataveillance even more effective. The Electronic Privacy Information Centre (EPIC) has successfully persuaded many organisations, both public and commercial, not to divulge any SSNs they may legitimately hold. EPIC advise people to keep their SSN private since it is often 'the key to large amounts of personal information, including tax information, credit information, school records, and medical records'.

At present, it appears that the possibility of computer errors and the resulting false data is the price we have to pay for the little privacy still afforded to the individual in the information age. The business world is as keen as governments to acquire as much information on the public as it can.

Market research has flourished as an industry in recent years, and corporate databanks have continued to grow, becoming what are now referred to as 'data warehouses' – large computers that hold as much information as several large city libraries.

The data warehouse can be a valuable tool for corporate managers in making decisions on a wide range of situations. As an example, consider the catchment area covered by a chain of stores. If the store's owners knew the address of every customer, they could fine-tune their store building programme to ensure that the number of potential customers is maximised for the minimal outlay. They would try to avoid having stores so close together that their catchment areas overlapped, and would also avoid leaving any large concentration of potential customers uncovered. Possession of the customer addresses in a central databank would enable this analysis, improve the efficiency of the stores and would provide, ultimately, a better and cheaper service for the consumer.

Not many people give out their home address when buying goods from a shop. In order to get these addresses, many outlets in the UK are now asking their customers to give their postcode and house numbers at the till. The 'PC World' chain instruct their counter assistants to tell people that the postcode is necessary 'for VAT' (UK sales tax), and to back this up, their point-of-sale software will not print up the amount of VAT unless the customer divulges his or her address to the store. Other stores will claim that the address is needed 'for the guarantee'. This is all nonsense – the only products that a customer is obliged to give an address for is controlled items, such as firearms, or dangerous items such as poisons. The same applies to the US and other countries.

Corporate databanks use the combination of name and address to uniquely identify consumers and consequently build up detailed profiles of their spending habits. These profiles are either used internally or sold, at a considerable profit, to third parties.The public face of these activities is one of efficiency – understanding the needs and desires of the consumer. However, possession of intimate details of a person's spending habits can also be misused to direct and manipulate consumers into buying goods and services that they do not really need.

On the Web it is even easier for corporations to gather information on consumers. Many corporate web sites will deny access to new visitors until they have filled in an online form giving details about themselves. Most profit-oriented web sites collect and record the email address of every visitor. There are also computers on the Web that have been programmed to do nothing but ceaselessly search the Web looking for email addresses. These addresses are compiled into enormous mailing lists, which can contain up to 50 million email addresses, which are then sold on to direct marketing companies. As a result, the Web is awash with electronic junk mail, which is known as 'spam'.

Millions of junk emails are sent each day, advertising products and services that are often illegal. Products such as pornography, and 'services' such as chain letters, hoax appeals for donations to bogus good causes, and pyramid selling schemes. These spams rarely offer products or services that are genuinely targeted at the recipient. Even politicians have entered into the realm of junk email – in Autumn 1996, millions of people who had no interest or involvement were urged to vote Republican or vote Democrat in the US Presidential elections. When in possession of a huge mailing list, it is often simpler and cheaper to just email the advertisement to everyone on the list, rather than waste any time and money attempting to target an audience.

Spam mail is exclusive to the Web, and is bringing about its own threat to personal privacy, as email addresses are harvested, shared and sold, and mailboxes are invaded and all but overwhelmed. There is so much advertising sent by email that the entire system is becoming clogged up, infuriating users and increasing the costs for everyone. The situation is similar to one that appeared when fax machines became popular. Faxes would be flooded with faxed advertisements making them next to useless. The situation persisted until the practice of sending unsolicited faxes was made illegal.

The issue of privacy is a major topic of discussion, and heated debate, not only among Internet users but also at the highest levels of government, corporations, civil liberties groups, and international regulatory bodies. The European Union is leading the way to make provision of legal safeguards and unusually, the UK is at the forefront, having enacted the Data Protection Act as long ago as 1984. This UK law has recently been strengthened and updated to comply with the European Union's Directive on the 'Protection Of Individuals With Regard To The Processing Of Personal Data And On The Free Movement Of Such Data.' Many of the new constitutions written in this decade, such as those of Hungary and South Africa, specifically cite privacy as a right and many other countries around the world are drafting legislation to protect personal privacy. According to James Glave of Wired, the well known web site and magazine: 'more than 40 countries around the world have enacted, or are preparing to enact, laws that protect the privacy and integrity of personal consumer data.'

In stark contrast, the US has no single legal provision for the protection of privacy or any constitutional safeguards. Unlike the Europeans, Americans regard privacy and freedom of speech as conflicting ideals. A somewhat illogical situation has resulted, where it may be illegal for law enforcement to wiretap a telephone conversation, but an email conversation may be freely bugged without permission being required – even though it is carried along the same wires. The situation becomes less clear when one considers a phone call made over the Web. Can this call be wiretapped without permission, when an ordinary call cannot? The answer appears to be yes. If the call uses the Web then in a strict legal sense it is not a telephone conversation.

There have been several attempts to introduce up-to-date legislation in the US that covers the Web. However, each attempt has met with disaster; civil liberties groups and the public both becoming enraged as they regard it as Washington's bid to secure the technology of mass surveillance as its own. At present, the US government's policy is that personal privacy on the Web should be self-regulated by the industry. It has produced guidelines for web sites that collect information and regards this as adequate consumer protection. This is despite the fact that the US government is in possession of figures proving that the guidelines are largely ignored.

The present situation is one of confusion. The legal protection of private information in the US falls far short of European Union standards and doubts have been raised as to whether it is now legal for a multi-national corporation to transfer its internal data from the EU to North America. The EU's data privacy directive requires member states to prevent data travelling to non-EU states that do not provide an adequate level of protection. The US does not provide anything like the level of protection required by the EU and it has no plans to introduce any EU-style laws. Rather, the US is opposing such laws, adamant that it does not need them.

The privacy afforded by the new European laws only protects individuals from legitimate data users, such as the private and public sectors. Although they are intended to also protect against mass or routine surveillance, investigative departments of governments have a poor track record in abiding by their own rules. Most importantly, these laws do little to protect against the third and final group that are invading people's privacy on the Web: members of the public themselves. Stalkers, hackers, blackmailers, extortionists, con men, disgruntled employees, ex-lovers, aggrieved customers, and the simply nosy are all taking advantage of the Web's insecurities for revenge, profit or thrills. Personal computers are dreadfully insecure and whenever they are attached to the Web they become exposed to an international underground community waiting to put other people's computers to their own nefarious uses.

All this would make the Web seem like an insecure and dangerous place to be, rather than the exciting, informative invention it is billed as. These fears about security and privacy on the Web are not unfounded. The Web is insecure; products that can enhance its security are being outlawed and governments, in particular the US government, are proposing new laws that deny privacy and will keep the Web insecure for many years to come. It is left to individuals to provide their own security and, fortunately, this is not as difficult as it seems. There are abundant resources on the Web which people can use to ensure that their activities remain private. With a little understanding of the risks it soon becomes possible even for the novice user to take control of the information he or she puts out on to the Web. The remainder of this book will explain those risks, how they have come about, and what the user can do to minimise them and thus enjoy the benefits of the Web in private.

Net Spies

HOW INFORMATION SLIPS THROUGH
THE NET

As soon as a computer is connected to the Web, it may present a threat to privacy. Everything that a person does on the Web, every email message, every web page visited, every file downloaded, every conversation, is recorded somewhere. Frequently these activities are recorded in several places, and for many different reasons. System administrators log activity for security and performance analysis. Government agencies intercept Web traffic for automated mass surveillance. Direct marketers build detailed consumer profiles. Swindlers compile and share lists of 'suckers', and hackers break into machines.

Whatever a person does on the Web it will be less secure, and less private, than what they may choose to do in public. The Web, however, is often perceived as an anonymous medium, but this is not the case. Sending a personal email message has the 'feel' of a private activity – it can often be an intimate sharing of feelings that we would not want to broadcast to others. The structure of the Web, however, and the method of moving its messages from Point A to Point B is only a little more secure – and is sometimes less secure – than a public broadcast.

The Web can broadcast details of your personal affairs to all and moreover, the 'record' button has been pressed. Recording, archiving, and, recently, automated content analysis is possible by what government spokespeople will often refer to as 'highly advanced artificial intelligence enhanced computer brains'. Or some other evasive terminology that governments are wont to issue rather than admitting that 'we're not telling you about this'. Alternatively, such procedures are referred to as 'CLASSIFIED' – a secret service euphemism, perhaps for 'our own privacy'. But the Web does not discriminate.

The so-called Secret Services that maintain public web sites are themselves a favourite target of hackers who thrive upon the public humiliation of the state's own security specialists. The section of the FBI assigned to White House security had their pagers hacked into in April 1998. Some unknown person kept a transcript of their messages and, amid a flurry of White House denials and general press merriment, he or she published the FBI 'security' messages on the Web.

Extracts from these messages (edited for this book to remove information and telephone numbers that could be used to identify members of the public) follow. It provides fascinating insight into the shady inner world of White House security:

EAGLE CALL I MR BOB DOLE I HOLDING CALL

POTUS IS RESTING AT 3:50PM.

BOB WHEELOCK OF GOOD MORNING AMERICA (202) ###-####

CALL TAMMIE AT ###-####. SHE IS LOCKED OUT OF THE ROOM /NO KEY IS AT THE HOTEL

MEET ROADRUNNER FOR PAGER AND SURV. KIT JAYSON IS IN R/R GREGG SENDS

EAGLE ARRIVE I FOSTER I STADIUM...OP85

THE NAME ALSO PROVIDES GOODEN TO ASK EAGLE IF HE WANTS THE CALL

WHAT IS YOUR LOCATION, 1ST LADY WAITING. OP36.

YOUR CAR IS BEING TOWED FROM MC SITE. RETURN ASAP.

GREAT ROOM! YOUR FAMILY GOT A GREAT TOUR OF AF-1.

THIS IS A TEST OF AF-1 GROUP PAGE. REQUESTED BY CDR RICHARDS.

GO TO THE RON SECURITY ROOM FOR A PROBLEM.

IF YOU DON'T COME BACK WITH 6 OF THOSE T-SHIRTS X-LARGE DON'T COME TO THE SWBD.

SCHMUCK, HOW'S IT HANGIN??? TOOTLES...

HAVE PAPER FOR THE SPEACH (sic) WRITER IN HUB

HOTEL.

EVERYTHING GOING CO DIAL TO AND FROM TRIP SITE, OUR ESCAPE PLAN IN EFFECT.

CALL HOME FOR JOKE OF THE HOUR, KAY SENDS.

CALL YOUR MOTHER...OP142.

STAFF OFC FAX NEED TONER.

IF YOU DON'T COME BACK WITH FOOD...DON'T COME BACK—AIRBORNE!!!

ARE U THINKING OF ME BECAUSE I AM THINKING OF U!...01

CALL ME IF U CAN.I HAVE A 2 HR PHONE WATCH, #####...MISS U01

DON'T FORGET TO PAGE ME TONIGHT WHEN YOU WANT ME IN YOUR ROOM.

MINOR HOSTAGE SITUATION IN TEXAS...NOT MUCH KNOWN NOW...WILL ADVISE...

BEEP BEEP BEEP BEEP BEEP BEEP BEEP BEEP BEEP BEEP BEEP BEEP BEEP BEEP.

EAGLE DEPART I FOSTER I STADIUM I ENROUTE I WYND-HAM I HOTEL...OP85 I

WHERE R U?? R WE STILL GOING TO EAT???

I HAVE THE PRINTER FOR SPEACH (sic) WRITER IN COMCEN. WHAT ROOM #?

WHERE THE SIDEWALK ENDS THE ROAD BEGINS...

USSS WANTS THE RYDER TRUCK MOVED FROM THE 17TH STREET ENTRANCE.

PLEASE BRING LIMO KIT TO 2503

WILL BE OUT OF PFC FOR 20 MIN OR SO, GOING TO GET DRUNK - DAN.

I AM IN ROOM 918 IF I CAN BE OF ANY MORE HELP.I HAD A GREAT TIME! THANKS MUCH

CALL K. HICKMAN AT DROP34236.

YOU ARE VERY CUTE!!!

EAGLE CALL CHELSEA CLINTON HOLDING, PLEASE CALL SIGNAL OP 142.

MRS CHELSEA AND MRS CLINTON TALKING AT THIS
TIME.
RECIEVING LINE BACK STAGE AFTER SHOW.
TRY NOT TO DROOL ON TOO MANY PEOPLE, AND
REMEMBER I MISSU!!!
I GUESS I AM GOING TO SLEEP AND DREAM ABOUT
U...01
G WHERE ARE YOU? ARE YOU ALIVE?

Clearly an exciting time is had by all. The two agents
that were using their pagers to arrange clandestine meet-
ings of an illicit and possibly intimate nature suffered
deep personal embarrassment. Most embarrassed of all
must have been the (then) Head of White House security,
upon whom befell the unenviable duty of trying to explain
it all away in front of an ominously attentive press conference.

If the President of the United States of America, the
most powerful man in the whole wide world, otherwise
known as Mr. Big (as Monica allegedly wrote in a poorly
secured email) can't maintain his privacy – and it is by
now abundantly clear that he could not – then what hope
is there for the rest of us? Are all details of our lives, our
actions, our opinions even, to become public property?
The lack of privacy provided by the Web begs the question: why is such a pervasive medium so insecure? To
understand why this is so, we must look into the structure and development of the Web.

The world is ringed with communications systems.
Telephone cables, microwave towers, undersea cables,
satellites, radio, and television. The list continues to grow.
These systems are owned and operated by governments,
private corporations, and private individuals. Since
personal computers came onto the market in 1981, there
has been a trend to attach computers to existing commu-

nications networks to enable them to share information, and computing resources. An obvious example is the network printer, which is shared between many computer users. Many organizations from single-building offices all the way up to global corporations were connecting all of their computers onto their own private network.

The Web, which is purely software driven and virtually cost free, appeared in the early 1990s. It was a suite of programs that used Internet technology to share information. The Internet had been used by academics since the late sixties. The name is from the words 'inter' (between) and 'net' (networks). It is literally a system that connects networks together. Composed of software, it cheaply and efficiently uses existing communications infrastructure to massively expand the scope and effectiveness of earlier private computer networks.

Internet technology, now the industry standard, allows two or more networks to be connected to each other with little more effort than a telephone call. Messages arrive at their destination under the control of complex routing software that can navigate a route through the ever-changing complexity of so many interconnected networks.

The most popular method of accessing the Internet is through the Web using software called 'web browsers' (such as Netscape or Microsoft Internet Explorer). Indeed, to many people the World Wide Web is the Internet and the terms are now largely used interchangeably. It is a view of the Internet that is becoming close to reality as the Web subsumes all prior forms of communication both on and off the networks, and offers the potential to fully exploit proposed high capacity communications. The Web delivers electronic documents, which may include photographs, recorded or live video, CD quality music, or radio services.

Net Spies

Originally intended as a document sharing system for use over the Internet, the Web has quickly established itself as the easiest way to access the Internet. It – the Internet – has been described as 'the fastest growing invention in history'. It has seen remarkable growth during the Nineties but in fact it has existed since the late Sixties. The massive growth of the Internet during the Nineties was largely due to the introduction of the software that powers the Web – so-called webservers. It is these webservers that hold and distribute the information that is stored on the Web. They automatically deliver (or serve) requested web pages on demand to user operated web browsers. Until very recently most webserver machines were expensive items operated by businesses. Now, as computer power has risen, many private users are setting up their own personal webservers.

It is the web browser software that is used to access the Web, and it is through browsers that the Web is viewed. The first browser, called Mosaic, was distributed free of charge. It could do little more than display text with only rudimentary typesetting, and graphic images – which by today's standards seems somewhat banal, but it should be noted that formatted text and pictures are the only resources available to more traditional sources of public information books and periodicals.

Within a year of the release of Mosaic, in 1995, the number of users of the WWW increased dramatically, rising to tens of millions. In a short period of time a massive demand had arisen from almost nowhere. As often happens in computing, demand for a new service or product can suddenly appear in the marketplace, with the usual result that corporations exploit it for astronomical profit. The demand for business computers in the Fifties and Sixties was tapped into by what soon became the world's largest corporation: IBM. In the early 1980s, microprocessor and memory prices had fallen to levels low enough to offer home users powerful, easy to use computers.

The home market was also exploited by the previously unknown Apple Corporation who was the first manufacturer to place graphical user interfaces onto the desktop. Apple quickly became the fastest growing company in history earning, almost overnight, staggering sums of money for its founders Steve Wozniak and Steven Jobs. Less than ten years later, it was the little known Microsoft Corporation that performed a similar brand of commercial sorcery with the release of the Windows operating system. Windows soon came to dominate the market, earning in the process one of the most stupendous personal fortunes ever amassed for the founder and workaholic chairman of Microsoft, Bill Gates.

The intense competition for a share of the WWW market has led to modern browsers becoming extremely powerful. The development of technology has been astounding – only three years after their introduction, web pages were able to display high quality text and graphical layout, real-time sound, live and recorded video, online gaming, chat lines, and even video conferencing and telephone services. Web pages can also contain powerful software that allows users to interact with remote computers. The most significant aspect of this sort of interaction is that it has enabled commerce over the Internet. Web pages may take the place of the glossy mail order catalogues – so many of which go unread to the waste paper basket.

For many, the explosive appearance of such power and versatility heralded the true arrival of the much-hyped 'information age'. We were able to buy our software and have it instantly delivered from the comfort of our armchair. We became able to book flights, order and purchase consumer goods, read and even watch the news, all with our web browser software. Soon we will be able to buy and download CD quality music and digital television in real-time, and instantly and cheaply make a video-phone call anywhere in the world. The information culture is upon us in the form of the Web and it is rapidly defining itself as the dominant communications medium for the next century. Such was the emergence, and the continuing hype, of this complex and intangible new invention; the information superhighway.

In the rush to get onto and exploit the Web, the related notions of security and privacy have been largely overlooked. Much of the security of the Web now relies upon ad hoc design and retrospectively fitted 'enhancements'. Much of the security now on offer is widely regarded as, at best, insufficient. It has been left to the operators of the individual networks that, together, form the Internet to adopt their own security practices. A primary role of all network administrators is the protection of their own networks. Consequently many networks are well secured, but many others are not, and some networks are positively hostile and should be avoided at all costs, but it is often difficult to judge who really owns a given network.

A valuable tool for network security is the system log. This is a file that records whatever details of user activity that the administrator wishes. Systems logs have been used as evidence in cases of illegal computer intrusion. They identify who has accessed a machine and what they did while they were there. The economic value of the information contained in such system logs, particularly those that log web page accesses, was also quickly recognised and exploited. Web search services can collate massive quantities of consumer data that has a high market value. The most popular web sites are those that offer so-called 'search engines'. These are interactive web pages that allow people to rapidly search a large part of the Internet for any words or phrases they desire. Some of these search services are extremely powerful and greatly simplify navigation of the Web. A brief discussion of how search engines, work provides a useful insight into how data is harvested, processed, and turned into profit.

Web pages that offer search engines are data entry screens for requesting information from a database. The database program runs on the search service provider's system. This database contains copies of the text of millions of web pages that are available on computers all over the world. When a visitor enters a search term into the search engine the database is searched within seconds and a list of pages containing a match for the required term is displayed in the visitor's web browser, in the form of hypertext links. It is possible to search through many millions of pages so rapidly because the search engine is typically running on a very powerful computer. The providers of search engines also run programs known as 'spiders'. These programs simulate a person browsing the Web by following every link it can find and copying the text of the pages it visits into the database.

Search services are expensive to provide. Companies that provide the more powerful services free of charge are typically large computer manufacturers. One of the ways they can justify the expense of the service is through the enhancement of the product and brand awareness – advertising. Another advantage of providing the service is that it attracts large numbers of people and their data can provide opportunities for research and development. Possibly most valuable of all, though, is the information that the service can record whenever the service is used. Every word or phrase that is searched for is recorded, along with the network address of the person performing the search. Take into account that the most popular search engines receive hundreds of thousands of requests per day and it quickly becomes apparent what a vast resource this data represents.

This information is a valuable resource that can, and often is, sold on to third parties. Consider, for example, a music publishing company that mounts an advertising campaign for three new recording artists. That company will be interested in finding out which of those artists is generating the most public interest. This is something that could be revealed by examining the data in Internet search engines. A sudden increase in searches for a promoted artist could prove invaluable in judging the effectiveness of the marketing campaign. Most of the larger search services are now, after much public pressure, removing any information that could identify individuals from the data they trade in. Recently in Europe it has become largely illegal to trade in data that can identify consumers. Almost all webservers keep a record of all visits to their pages. Most of these logs are benign, used by conscientious administrators who respect the privacy of their users.

An activity of webservers that has caused considerable privacy concerns is the practice of using 'cookies' to record potentially private information. A 'cookie' is a small file of information that a webserver is able to place onto a user's computer. By doing so, the webserver is able to 'remember' things about visitors. For example, you may regularly make purchases from the web pages of an online store. It might be inconvenient and off-putting if you had to enter your name and address for delivery of the goods on each visit. To make the pages more user-friendly, a 'cookie' could be stored on your computer that the store's webserver can refer to every time you return.

How Information Slips Through the Net

This sounds like a useful feature, and since the information is stored on a person's own computer it is difficult, at first, to envisage any potential for privacy violation. As Steven Segal, a writer on computing issues, puts it, 'Be prepared for a shock about the amount of information stored. I knew something about cookies for a while, but never gave them much attention until an odd thing happened. I noticed something amiss when I visited the Web site of the Yahoo! search engine and clicked on the "Local Yahoo!" link. Yahoo knew my home ZIP code, yet I had not typed it in. I was puzzled as to how it knew this information. Then, it occurred to me that I had typed in this information several weeks ago and Yahoo! had somehow remembered.'

On large, content rich web sites, cookies can be used to track a user's progress through the site. The user's preferences, likes and dislikes, and any details he or she may volunteer can all be stored in the cookie. Huge numbers of such cookies then become a valuable market research resource that direct marketers and cold callers will pay large sums of money for.

It is also possible for 'badly behaved' sites to adapt cookies to enable them to record a user's subsequent actions, even after they have moved on to other web sites. Any information entered by the user, such as usernames or passwords, could – in theory – be recorded by the cookie and later retrieved by the offending web site.

The use of cookies only appeared with the more modern browsers and, for users who are concerned, it is possible to 'switch them off'.

With modern browsers there is an even more worrying possibility: it is demonstrably possible for an eavesdropper to intercept and take complete control over everything that passes between the browser and the server.

Net Spies

'Web spoofing' is a form of security threat where an eavesdropper creates a false, but in every way identical, image of the entire Internet. This is a lot easier than it sounds – the eavesdropper intercepts your activities and processes them for you. For example, when a user clicks upon a hypertext link to view another page, the eavesdropper will intercept the request. Once intercepted, the eavesdropper can collect the requested web page and pass it back to the user that made the request. This gives an eavesdropper a complete and undetectable record of everything the user does on the network. It allows for the interception of all requests for pages, the contents of any forms that are filled in while online – including passwords, credit card numbers, or other personal information. It is also a method that defeats any of the presently available 'secure server' technology.

Secure servers were created to allay public fears about the lack of security and privacy on networks. There are several competing methods currently in use to provide secure transactions over the Web but all are, in principle, based in the same idea; they are all based upon encryption. Any personal information sent from the user to the server is encrypted with a secret password known only to the browser and server. This is a transparent operation that enables secure pages to maintain the same ease of use as unsecured pages. When a user requests pages from a secure server, the browser and the server will first negotiate a password which they will then use to encrypt and decrypt the information they pass between each other. There are now many sites offering such security for services ranging from online transactions to the remote collection of email.

Secure servers do not protect against web spoofing. The program being run by the eavesdropper will be acting as a server as far as the user's browser is concerned.

Indeed, for the interception to be successful it must act identically to a server. When the site discovers a request for a secure page it must negotiate a password with the browser itself. It will then collect the information from the secure server by negotiating a second password with that server. So, the eavesdropper is swapping information with the user by using one code, and swapping information with the secure server using another. To both the secure server and the user, this appears to be completely normal operation. The eavesdropper is able to decode any encrypted information sent by the user. This problem is not limited to simple eavesdropping either. It is also possible for any eavesdropper to tamper with and modify any information that it acquires.

Web spoofing attacks such as these were demonstrated in February 1997 by a team of researchers at Princeton University. The attack was carried out in a way in which it was undetectable to all but a suspicious expert. At present, the Internet is susceptible to this kind of spying on individuals whereby every piece of information that passes between the individual's PC and the network may be recorded. Web spoofing may be used for fraudulent purposes, but it is a method that is fairly easy to trace once it has been detected.

In cases of surveillance, there is no reason to suppose that it would be detected, whereas fraud is almost certainly going to be detected and investigated. Web spoofing is therefore a tactic best suited to eavesdropping and is unlikely to be used for fraud.

In fact, web spoofing is something of a game. An eavesdropper cannot single out a specific individual for surveillance and begin monitoring their activities. Before any monitoring can begin, the eavesdropper must first lure the individual into viewing a page that contains the necessary programs. Once this has been achieved, that user can be spoofed (or watched) until they close down their browser software. There are many ways in which a user can be lured onto a web site – a direct email invitation is an obvious method – and the larger the organisation the easier it will be since they will have a wider range of sites on offer. Web spoofing is an ideal method by which large scale corporations, law enforcement agencies and security services can monitor the online activities of targeted individuals.

As with most security risks, the defence against web spoofing relies on a little understanding of the problem. As described above, the spoofing cannot begin until an eavesdropper's site has been viewed and it ends when the browser is shutdown (or when the eavesdropper is satisfied or bored enough to relinquish control). So those who suspect they may be being spied upon need only shutdown and restart their browser to cut off the eavesdropper.

To ensure the contact with those sites that require the sharing of personal or sensitive information remains private, it is best to visit such sites immediately after starting up your browser, so that it is the first page you visit. This will ensure that your browser will not be spoofed and that your personal details will be seen only by yourself and the site you have given them to.

The ever-increasing power of computers is extending the range of services the Web can provide, but it is also making it less secure. Home and desktop computers have only recently acquired the computing power necessary to begin fully exploiting the potential of the Web. Commercial operating systems such as Microsoft Windows 95, or Linux (a system similar to UNIX available for downloading from the Web free of charge), provide computer users with considerable power and flexibility. Both of these systems, and others, provide users with a graphically based 'point and click' environment that supports networking and audio-visual multimedia enhancements.

Interconnectivity and multimedia are the capabilities that transform low-cost personal computer systems into ideal vehicles with which to cruise the Web. It is also the power that can turn such computers into shockingly intrusive surveillance devices that anyone, worldwide, can tap into. Attach a microphone to such a computer and it becomes a low-cost telephone – or an audio bugging device, depending on how it is used. Upgrade a PC for video conferencing – and give everyone on the Web the chance to watch and record what you are doing in what used to be the privacy of your own home.

In August 1998, such threats to personal privacy were highlighted by a group of self-proclaimed 'security conscious' hackers calling themselves 'The Cult of the Dead Cow'. They released a virus-like program onto the Web, aimed at users of Windows 95 which, so they claim, 'draws attention to security flaws in modern operating systems'.

The program, called Back Orifice (BO), which is mockingly named after Microsoft's 'Back Office' suite of programs, effectively turns infected machines into public access computers. It is a sophisticated, and admittedly well produced, network administration tool, which could in certain circumstances be used positively. It can also be used for far more sinister purposes, and it is that aspect of the program that led to a storm of publicity that forced a statement from the mammoth Microsoft Corporation. Back Orifice is not a program that can be bought in the shops. It is a program written by hackers and distributed on the Web for free. And, under these conditions, it can easily be misused for invasive, nefarious purposes, with no questions asked.

Computers that have BO installed upon them may be used by anyone on the Internet without the owner's knowledge or consent. Alternatively, it may be configured to give a sole person complete and anonymous control of the infected computer – without that person even having to be on the same continent as the keyboard.

BO spreads in a similar manner to a computer virus and silently installs itself onto computer systems using the same techniques that virus writers have been using for many years. In the words of the writers it is 'entirely self installing' – a tongue-in-cheek hacker's euphemism for 'virus'. Unlike a virus, however, this program does not directly cause damage to the computers it infects. But it can be used to cause any level of harm that the malicious user intends, as BO grants full access to the infected computer to any person that detects the infection. Moreover, it is designed so that the infected machines advertise their infection on the Web. Once detected, malicious users may use that computer for any purpose just as if they were sat at its keyboard. All files on the infected computer are made available to the intruder. It can also send the intruder – or anyone else for that matter – a complete transcript of everything the owner types at the keyboard, including passwords, and it allows intruders to run any program on the infected computer. This is a dangerous and powerful attack on the security, privacy, and integrity of online systems.

It has to be said, though, that The Cult of Dead Cow are hackers with a conscience. This program is easily removed – it was added to virus databases within weeks of release – and it serves the function of truly highlighting just how insecure personal computers are. Software manufacturers, such as Microsoft, claim that they are aware of security, and they provide the means for customers to protect themselves. This is true, but security has a price attached to it that is measured in more than pounds and pence (or dollars and cents if you prefer). Most operating systems are delivered, and installed, in a default configuration that is woefully inadequate for securing the user's privacy. Naturally vendors will sell you security enhancements at a price, but often these do little more than the features that come with the computer but which are turned off in the default installation.

It is left very much up to the user to turn on and monitor these features, but this is something that will typically involve wading through a pile of 'user guides' written in 'technobabble', which is no doubt off-putting to the average computer user.

A good example of such can be found on The Cult of the Dead Cow's official web site. They describe (or market?) BO as, 'a remote administration system which allows a user to control a computer across a tcpip connection using a simple console or GUI application. On a local LAN or across the Internet, BO gives its user more control of the remote Windows machine than the person at the keyboard of the remote machine has. BO is small, and entirely self installing. Simply executing the server on any Windows machine installs the server, moving the executable into the system where it will not interfere with other running applications. To ease distribution, BO can also be attached to any other Windows executable, which will run normally after installing the server. Once running, BO does not show up in the task list or close program list, and is rerun every time the computer is started. The filename that it runs as is configurable before it is installed, and it's as easy to upgrade as uploading the new version and running it.'

In effect, they are saying that once installed on a remote machine, it may be used to open the machine to the world and make available to all, every bit of stored data and resources. It is incredible what an intruder can achieve using BO; arbitrary messages may be displayed on the victim's screen, the intruder may inspect and delete any file on the computer, obtain passwords, send and receive email, connect to other machines, run arbitrary programs, and log every keystroke made by the victim. In essence, an intruder can use the victim's 'orificed' computer for any task or purpose that that computer is capable of without the victim ever being aware of what is happening.

Most people would naturally take offence to a stranger reading their email and personal files, regarding this as an invasion of privacy. To victims of BO, however, this is just the tip of the iceberg. Modern multimedia PCs often have microphones, and sometimes video cameras attached. An intruder can use BO to access these devices and very effectively bug the victim, recording and maybe even viewing, everything that happens in the room where the compromised machine is located. The KGB could only have dreamed of possessing a tool to give such comprehensive powers of surveillance. The Internet combined with high-speed multimedia technology places this power into the hands of the general public. Back Orifice works by intercepting the messages that pass between the Windows 95 software and the PC hardware. In this way it is able to effectively take control, or listen in on, all of the devices attached to the infected PC; the keyboard, the microphone, the speakers, the disk. Everything that isn't physically disconnected from the PC can come under the control of BO.

At the time of writing, over 100,000 copies of BO have been downloaded. Estimates of the number of 'orificed' computers are in the tens of thousands. The BO password protection device, however, can make it hard to detect, so the true extent of its proliferation is unknown. BO is, however, relatively easy to detect if you have access to the PC. Anyone who thinks they may be infected can simply use any of the many freely available anti-virus programs that are distributed over the Web.

An intruder using BO may actually have no interest in the personal details of the victim. Instead the intent of the intrusion is often to simply use the victim's identity. Identity theft is common on computer networks. Malicious hackers and criminals cover their tracks by using many intervening machines between their own and the target they are attacking. The logging capabilities of computers facilitate the detection and tracking down of intruders. Consequently hackers often gain access to a poorly-secured machine to use that to attack their real target. The real target of the hackers could be anything; pranksters hoping to write graffiti on the FBI Home Page; an office worker trying to break into the email box of the woman in the next office whom he secretly desires; the DEA looking for evidence of drugs trafficking; hi-tech thieves after credit card numbers; maybe someone is just 'having a nose around'. There are almost as many reasons why people want to hack into computers as there are computers. Back Orifice demonstrates how easy it can be.

The security mechanisms on a computer so hacked, by proxy as it were, will then log the intervening machine as being the source of the attack. Of course it is possible that the owner of the intervening machine may be able to trace the source of the original intrusion, but to do so requires detailed knowledge of networking software and protocols, not to mention the knowledge that their machine has been used in the first place. Because a malicious hacker would be able to alter any of the log files, so removing all traces of the intrusion. In the worst case scenario, an intruder may simply delete everything stored on an attacked computer to erase all traces of illegal activity, which in itself would not go unnoticed. It would, however, be practically impossible to discover who performed the deletion.

Fortunately, BO is fairly easy to detect and remove before too much damage is done. Since it spreads like a virus, it can be detected by anti-virus software. What is more difficult to prevent is the intrusion of hackers – and others from gaining access to a computer. Computers have been hacked into for far longer than the Web has existed. The telephone system was regularly hacked in the 1960s and 70s by so-called 'Phone Phreakers'. These were mainly electronics hobbyists exploiting the design of the telephone network to obtain free long distance calls. As the telephone network became computerised, the Phreakers became or were replaced by hackers who were soon able to break into almost any computer that is attached to a telephone line. Now computer and network security is big business – both for crooks and those trying to catch them. The hobby hacker is fast becoming an outlaw, demonised by investigators and sensationalised in the media.

Behind all of the anti-hacking hype, however, there are the extortionists that have received very little publicity. They are believed by Western police forces to have links with the Russian Mafia, and they are breaking into business computers and holding them to ransom, threatening to wipe out all business data unless money is paid. A spokesman for the Metropolitan Police in London says that in 1998 'a sum running into possibly hundreds of millions of pounds has been extorted in this way. Most companies cough up rather than risk losing customer confidence by admitting that their computers have been broken into.' He has a point. Would you place your trust in a company that cannot even protect its own assets? This is a problem that is only now beginning to be acknowledged and nobody is quite sure as to the true extent of the losses involved.

It is left to the hobby hackers – mostly highly skilled programmers – to bring the appalling lack of computer security to the attention of the public. It is worrying to think that there is so little security on computer networks. If hobbyist programmers are able to gain full access to a private machine, one wonders just what powers of surveillance are available to investigators armed with State resources. State surveillance of computer networks is the subject we shall turn our attention to next.

Footnotes

1 POTUS - President of the United States

2 SWBD - switchboard

3 USSS - United States Secret Services

Net Spies

WHO'S WATCHING YOU?

For many years, any suggestion that the government was bugging every telephone in the land would have been dismissed as paranoia or as a conspiracy theory. Sceptics would reason that it would be an impossible waste of resources to monitor all telephone calls. The better-informed sceptic would perhaps produce persuasive figures, convincing himself or herself that this just would not – could not – happen.

Doubtless there were many East German citizens that adopted and believed similar arguments. That is, until the collapse of the Communist government revealed that the state security forces, the infamous Stasi, had indeed installed a bug in every telephone outlet in East Germany. A microphone bug was attached to every telephone socket, as opposed to attached to the phone itself, so that they could listen in on all conversations in the room; not just those on the telephone. Essentially, the Stasi had simply used the telephone system as a cover for a massive covert surveillance network. The Stasi spying system was vast, with some 500,000 informers and over 10,000 employed simply to listen into and transcribe the conversations from the bugged telephone system.

From one point of view, it is fortunate that only ten per cent of the East German population were connected to the telephone network. But even so, the ability to instantly listen in on the activities in one tenth of the homes and businesses in the country must have seemed like a dream come true to East German security personnel.

Worryingly, such a bugging system now exists in Western countries. ISDN line telephones are rapidly replacing the older and more basic handset phones. This new technology provides the user with a whole host of new services, but what is less widely known is that the ISDN system allows a remote operator to activate the microphone so that it is effectively 'off-hook' in order to bug the room that the telephone is located in.

The sceptic we met a little earlier would reason that this new facility would never be abused in the West, and that no comparison can be drawn between the repressive activities of communist dictatorships with those of democratically elected Western governments. The cost in human resources alone would surely rule out this scale of surveillance, and given that almost everyone has a telephone, and in many cases, several telephones, most of the country would be employed in surveillance, so defeating the object of the exercise. Besides, mass surveillance is illegal in a free country.

Or is it? A report to the European Parliament entitled 'An Appraisal of Technologies of Political Control' does make one think again. The report, commissioned by the Civil Liberties Committee of the European Parliament, was published in December 1997 and it confirmed the existence of a huge electronic spy network that monitors all electronic communications in Europe. Every telephone call, every fax, and all data communications can and indeed are being indiscriminately monitored as a matter of routine.

The human resources required to perform the surveillance are no longer an issue as the spies, known in the trade as 'signals intelligence' (SIGINT) are simply banks of computers. Technology has existed since the 1970s that can transcribe spoken conversations, 'read' faxes, and so convert the content into a form that can be automatically analysed by 'intelligent' computer programs. Widespread use of email assists these electronic detectives because emails are, by their very nature, already in a form that the machines can utilise. This frees up system resources to allow the monitoring of an increasing proportion of the world's communications.

Messages are 'read' by computers that apply state-of-the-art techniques of artificial intelligence to perform content analysis. Their programmers having provided them with a dictionary of potentially suspicious names, words, and phrases, the SIGINT computers compile lists of all those communications that may be suspect. The names or numbers of the people concerned are then passed on to human operators who will decide whether closer investigation of the individuals involved is warranted.

Just who would be running such a spy network in Western Europe? Is this another example of Brussels intruding on British sovereignty? Is it run by the British Security Services? Is it a vital tool standing in defence of the British Isles? It is none of these. The installation is in fact the 13th USASA Field Station based at Menwith Hill in the north of England; an RAF site which the US Government leases from Britain. This is a cover; the installation is actually operated by the US National Security Agency and its exact purpose was until recently, a mystery. The site is part of a global US surveillance system known as Project P415.The Menwith Hill listening post is the largest installation of a global surveillance system operated by the US government with the co-operation of Canada, the United Kingdom, Australia, and New Zealand. These five nations pooled their intelligence resources during World War Two. After the war, in 1947, they signed the UKUSA agreement, which is still in operation. This secret treaty allows each of the five signatories to continue sharing intelligence, to use each other's intelligence gathering resources, and more sinisterly, it allows each nation to circumvent its own national laws in intelligence operations targeted against their own citizens.

Details of the surveillance carried out under UKUSA were revealed in New Zealander Nicky Hager's book entitled 'Secret Power'. Hager writes chiefly about New

Zealand's intelligence agency, the Government Communications Security Bureau (GCSB) which is their equivalent of the US National Security Agency. With help from over fifty current and former intelligence staff, Hager documents how the global ECHELON system is used to routinely – and indiscriminately – intercept email, faxes and telephone conversations.

The Menwith Hill base is conveniently located next to a strategic Post Office communications tower. It is one of five major 'listening posts' around the world. The spy stations are located to provide maximum coverage of the international communications network. This enables the US government and its spies to listen in to almost any electronic communications that take place anywhere in the world. The Earth is ringed by a network of international telecommunications satellites known as Intelsat. These sit high above the equator in geostationary orbit and relay tens of thousands of telephone calls, faxes, and email messages simultaneously. This network is spied upon by listening posts located at Morwenstow in Cornwall, Sugar Grove in West Virginia, the Yakima Firing Centre in Washington State, Waihopai in New Zealand, and Geraldton in Western Australia.

The location of these 'electronic ears' provides complete coverage of the Intelsat network. A separate network of listening posts monitor communications satellites that were put into place by the Soviet Union, and other nations that are, or have been considered hostile. These are at Shoal Bay, in Northern Territory, Australia; Leitrim, in Ottawa, Canada; Bad Aibling in Germany; Misawa in Japan; and the largest of all at Menwith Hill in the UK. There is also a large amount of telecommunications traffic that travels overland (by microwaves and cables) and along the seabed through cables that span the oceans. This traffic tends to converge on large cities and it is very easy for SIGINT operators to intercept. All that is required for surveillance is an ordinary building somewhere along the signal path, connected into the network by a hidden cable or microwave receiver. In London, for example, an anonymous red brick building located at 8 Palmer Street, is used by GCHQ for routinely intercepting and monitoring every telex passing through London. The contents of each telex is analysed by a dictionary computer, and anything deemed to be suspicious is automatically forwarded to one or more of the five partners that may be interested.

The purpose of the Palmer Street installation was revealed to Granada Television's World in Action documentary series team by an unnamed former GCHQ official. He told Granada that the monitoring of telecommunications is 'nothing to do with national security. It's because it's not legal to take every single telex. And they take everything: the embassies, all the business deals, even the birthday greetings, they take everything. They feed it into the Dictionary.' What the documentary did not reveal, or was perhaps prevented from revealing, is that this listening operation is carried out on behalf of the American National Security Agency (NSA) under the terms of the UKUSA agreement.

British researcher Duncan Campbell has revealed that the Post Office communications tower sited close to the Menwith Hill station is a key component of the telecommunications backbone in the UK.

Moreover, the tower is directly linked by wire to a secretive 'Dictionary' spy network. That Menwith Hill was awarded the NSA's coveted 'Station of the Year' award in 1991, recognising its role during the Gulf War, gives some idea of the scope and range of the listening devices it possesses.

The computers that perform this automated snooping

are known by the codename ECHELON, or 'The Echelon Dictionaries'. Each of the five 'dictionary' stations around the world has its own codename; for example, the Washington and Waihopai stations are known as COWBOY and FLINTLOCK respectively.

The United States National Security Agency routinely monitors all European telecommunications. But for what purpose? The ECHELON system dates back to the secret 1947 UKUSA Treaty, the aim of which was for the five member nations to co-operate in the development of a global intelligence organisation, sharing both common resources and common goals. During the Cold War, the prime purpose of ECHELON was to monitor the Soviet Union, a mission the West was prepared to spare no expense on.

The end of the Cold War promised significant cutbacks in defence spending throughout the Western world; the so-called 'peace dividend'. This led to defence departments having to fight to maintain their budget. Intelligence agencies had to justify the continuation of their funding from the taxpayer by re-focusing their attention towards terrorists and drug traffickers. The net result is that the military-industrial complex of the Cold War years has been transformed into a police-industrial complex in the Nineties. Intelligence services now operate to a new brief in their home territories, known as Operations Other Than War or Law Enforcement; which arguably alludes to an Orwellian nightmare in the making. In Great Britain, the branch of the Secret Service most obviously affected by the end of the Cold War was MI6, the department responsible for 'external security' – a euphemism for spying on foreign nations. The legality of MI6 investigating British citizens is questionable, as this role is normally carried out by the police or MI5. One of the beauties of the UKUSA agreement, however, is its reciprocity. Under the agreement, the US may spy on British citizens, and the UK in turn can spy upon Americans. Each nation in the agreement then pools the information gained and effectively they are achieving the goal of spying on their citizens without breaking any national laws designed to prevent such behaviour. As a result, both the US and the UK follow the strict letter of the law, while adopting a distinctly atheist stance towards the spirit of the law.

The dubious activities of the Menwith Hill listening station were detailed in Parliament in 1994 by Bob Cryer MP, member for Bradford South. Speaking during an adjournment debate, Mr Cryer began by reminding the government of a question he had been asking ministers for more than six years. It was a question that had never been satisfactorily answered, even though he had put it to a succession of defence ministers. He asked them to 'list the agreements authorising the use of Menwith Hill communications base, Harrogate, by the United States National Security Agency.' A long-time campaigner against the base, Cryer said: 'Its establishment has been accompanied by lies, evasion, deceit and a persistent refusal on the part of Ministers to provide proper information to elected representatives'

'In other words', continued Cryer, 'elected Members of Parliament are denied information on the appropriation of more than 200 acres of land by the United States Government, who now run a spy station in the heart of our country which is linked up to a global network. That is inexcusable. If there is parliamentary accountability, the moon is made of green cheese.'

He then detailed the initial purchase of the site by the US Army and its subsequent take over by the NSA after the Army objected to spying on civilians. Cryer described its current activities as 'a sophisticated version of a man in the dirty raincoat looking through a bedroom window or the pervert spying through a lavatory keyhole. Those who defend the station's invasion of our land, which has never been approved by parliament, are no better.'

Referring to unanswered questions he had put to ministers throughout the 1990s, he said, 'There is no glory or wonderful purpose involved in Menwith Hill. That is all the more true now that the Cold War is over. Ministers justified the Menwith Hill base by saying it was part of the Cold War, but we understand that that has finished. What is their justification for the spy station now?

One of the station's activities that the government must justify was; 'The fact that domestic intrusion exists at Menwith Hill station is surely shown by the fact that British Telecom has a 32,000-telephone capacity from Hunter's Stone Post Office tower along the B6451 [road] to Otley. There cannot be 32,000 telephones on the base in simultaneous use; that defies credibility.'

It should be noted that there were only around 1200 staff employed at the base, in itself a trebling of capacity since the end of the Cold War. 'The Hunter's Stone Post Office tower happens to be a pivotal point of more than 1 million route miles of microwave radio connections installed in Britain. The cable from Hunter's Stone Post Office tower runs directly to Menwith Hill. There has never been any parliamentary authority to allow this serious and unwarranted intrusion into our telephone network.'

Cryer then went on to comment on possible US commercial exploitation of the base. 'There are two large United States firms within the military-industrial complex: Loral Space Systems Incorporated, formerly a part of Ford, and Lockheed Aerospace. They sell much of the spy equipment and they are both involved in arms sales to third world countries. Menwith Hill gains information that would be useful to them. Lockheed and Boeing, for example, oppose the success of Airbus Industrie, which has sold many aeroplanes round the world. Can the minister guarantee that information about commercial matters relating to Airbus Industrie and the sales of the Airbus 300, for example, has never been picked up by Menwith Hill and has never been passed on to part of the US military-industrial complex? Both Boeing and Lockheed depend for their continued existence on military contracts from the United States Government.'

Howard Teicher, former head of the CIA cites a specific example of the commercial use of spy networks: 'The United States was always concerned about the purchase of non-American advanced armaments by the government of Saudi Arabia. We were certainly aware that by preventing a foreign government from selling something that we hoped would lead to an American entity to be able to sell, it would certainly contribute to our commercial interest.' That a foreign nation should be doing this with British resources on British territory prompted Cryer to accuse the then Conservative government of betraying the British people. 'Our Government', he said, 'continue to betray our people by allowing spy stations such as Menwith Hill to be dominated and operated by the United States, without any control that is visible to the people at large.'

In support of his opposition to the base he quotes former employees and victims of ECHELON. Margaret Newsham, a former Menwith Hill employee says, 'from the very beginning of my employment, it became very much aware to me that massive security violations were taking place. All the programs that I did work on were subject to these abuses.' Abdeen Jaburo, a US lawyer and victim of NSA surveillance, said 'It took me eighteen years to get my records finally destroyed. It is like Big Brother. It's like '1984', surveilling people all over the globe. And if you're

British, if you're French, if you're Dutch, you're any-any people, anywhere you have no rights to complain about this. You have zero rights.'

An employee of the NSA he quotes as saying: 'Menwith Hill was responsible for intercepting "ILC" and "NDC" traffic from 1966 to 1976. Then came the satellite intercepts, like MOONPENNY. ILC is "International Leased Carrier" – basically, ordinary commercial traffic. Your and my phone calls. And "NDC" is "Non-US Diplomatic Communications". But that job later moved out of Menwith Hill, during the 1970s to Chicksands, where a special unit called DODJOCC was run by the NSA, direct from Menwith Hill. DODJOCC stands for Department of Defence Joint Operations Centre Chicksands. Because of the high sensitivity of its work no Britons were ever allowed in.'

In plain English, translated from its native SIGINT gibberish, what he is in effect saying, is that 'ECHELON is used for commercial spying to give US corporations an unfair competitive advantage'.

Shortly after delivering this speech Mr Cryer, a committed and life-long peace campaigner, was tragically killed in a traffic accident. However, he concluded his speech by repeating the same questions that had met with, in his own words, 'lies, evasion, deceit and a persistent refusal on the part of ministers to provide proper information.'

The questions that remained largely unanswered for some years were: what is the first priority at Menwith Hill? Will the Minister publish the agreement that allows Menwith Hill to be operated at the base near Harrogate? Why should not the people of the United Kingdom know about these matters? What laws govern the operation of Menwith Hill? Do the United States employees there come under United Kingdom law or does the Visiting Forces Act 1952 apply to civilians? What rights do individuals or companies have if they believe that Menwith Hill is spying on them? For example, can the Minister give a categorical assurance that Menwith Hill is not intercepting commercial traffic?

The spy station at Menwith Hill has been known about for some time. The first report was as long ago as 1980 when New Statesman magazine published an article describing Menwith Hill as 'The Billion Dollar Phone Tap.' Armed Forces Ministers have spent years evading questions about Menwith Hill. The types of questions outlined above have prompted ministers of successive governments to answer – or rather to avoid answering – with unusual similarity.

When serving as Armed Forces Minister, Jeremy Hanley (Conservative) declined to answer with uncharacteristic frankness. 'The function of Menwith Hill station,' he told Bob Cryer, 'is regarded by Her Majesty's Government as being of the highest importance to the country's defence strategy and is subject to confidential arrangements between the UK and US Governments. The work carried out there is highly sensitive and rightly classified as secret.

'I believe very firmly that it would not be in the national interest, and would indeed defeat the very purpose of that work, if I were to comment in any detail on the activities that I have seen conducted there.' Labour Minister, Dr John Reid, then Minister for the Armed Forces was less forthcoming when replying to a written question put by backbench MP Mr. Baker, Junior Spokesperson on the Environment for the Liberal Democrats. In essence though, he agreed with his Conservative predecessor by not replying: 'I am withholding information on the operations of the intelligence and security agencies under exemption 1 of the Code of Practice on Access to Government Information on the grounds of national secu-

Net Spies

rity'. Earl Howe (Conservative) avoided the subject with ease: 'It is not government policy to comment on the detailed operations at RAF Menwith Hill'.

Can it really be in our national interest to allow the US government to bug our telephones for industrial espionage that benefits US companies at the expense of our own? How many European jobs are lost when US companies are provided with the sensitive, and private, commercial secrets of European companies? Is the British government, perhaps, gaining economic or political advantage from the surveillance it performs – as part of the reciprocity of the UKUSA agreement – on US communications? The first question that needs to be answered is just what this surveillance system is capable of.

During the Cold War, the primary purpose of Menwith Hill and its related stations was to spy on the communications of the Soviet Union and other 'hostile' powers. At that time most of the monitoring would have been performed by human listeners transcribing the communications of target individuals. Diplomatic telephone calls were considered highest priority and these would be intercepted routinely and transcribed by intelligent voice recognition software called Oratory. Faxes would have been analysed by optical character recognition (OCR) systems that could 'read' the text and compare it with the dictionary of suspicious words. Software such as this is available to the public and is becoming more and more reliable.

The cutting edge software available to security services is presumably even more advanced. For example, the so-called 'Ring of Steel' around London's financial district uses highly advanced software to monitor traffic. Whenever a car or motorcycle enters the City, surveillance cameras take a picture of the registration plate. The registration number is then 'read' by an OCR system and a request for information on the vehicle is sent to the online Police National Computer (PNC). If the PNC has listed the vehicle as 'suspicious' the surveillance system – which have complete coverage of the entire square mile – will follow concentrate on the suspect for the entire time that it remains within the Ring of Steel. A recent development that police forces are beginning to deploy is surveillance software that can recognise individual faces on closed circuit television systems. Doubtless the Menwith Hill station has been using systems at least as powerful as those described above to automatically spy upon a growing number or telephone and fax communications.

No such sophistication is necessary for the NSA to monitor, and analyse the content of Web communications. All communications on the Web are, by its very nature, already in a format suitable for computer analysis. Email is very often just plain text that may be directly compared to ECHELON's dictionaries. It requires relatively little computer resources to mass-monitor email and as the use of email has grown throughout the Nineties its employees must have been inundated with names of individuals that the Dictionary computers regard as 'suspicious'. Is it, then, any surprise that the number of staff employed at Menwith Hill has grown from 400 to 1800 since the end of the Cold War?

Government agents (or 'spooks' as they are commonly known) are not just watching the Web – they are also using it. When the British government accused ex-MI5 agent David Shayler of breaching the Official Secrets Act, he threatened to expose details of MI5 operations on a web site. He was held in prison in France for several months before the French courts rejected the British application for his extradition. On investigation, the network hosting Shayler's site also hosts the web pages of a company specialising in surveillance at rates 'as low as $30 per agent per hour'. It also hosts a Boston-based sex site, a direct marketing company, and a cultist site offering to sell 'Bible Reading Classes'. It appears as though, on the Web at least, Shayler is keeping with the company one might expect of an MI5 agent.

One investigator, who anonymously posts to the Web, has claimed that the company hosting Shayler's site is a front organisation of the CIA. If this is true then it is incredulous that an ex-MI5 agent should happen to choose it to host his illegal revelations of state secrets. On Shayler's unexpected release from prison in Paris the entire episode took on an air of disinformation. The Parisian backdrop to his imprisonment was quite likely linked to the secrecy of the investigation into the death of Diana, Princess of Wales. At about the same time as the Shayler affair, an alleged former CIA agent was arrested for attempting to sell 'secret papers' indicating a joint CIA/MI5 operation to cover up the circumstances of Diana's death.

Whether or not the Shayler episode was an official disinformation campaign, or merely the revenge of a disgruntled ex-employee, the fact that secret agents are out and about on the Web is clear. This is a fact that is also clear to Mark S., the owner of a Texan printing company that also was involved in the production of hemp paper from cannabis plants grown legally in California. Having spent time in prison for refusing to participate in the Vietnam War, Mark was suspicious that he would be considered a target for the security services. His suspicions were confirmed early in 1998, when he sent an email to a friend in Columbia in which he jokingly referred to killing the President. That same afternoon a group of FBI agents turned up at his printing firm for a full-scale search. Not having found anything illegal, the agents left.

But, before they did one of the agents advised, according to Mark, 'Be careful what you write in email'. No one should consider email private, but many people still do.

Even the infamous Starr Report, that in 1998 luridly chronicled the sex life of President Clinton, references the contents of private email messages sent by Monica Lewinksy. The FBI is pressuring to be allowed to listen in on private Web communications. It wants permission to access voice information sent over the Web without having to show reasonable grounds for suspicion that a telephone tap of the same individual would require. The Web is already being exploited by law enforcement agencies to circumvent laws put in place to protect the public.

It is not just government agents that are spying on people over the Web. To mark the 50th anniversary of the writing of George Orwell's "1984", the pressure group Privacy International organised the first annual Big Brother Awards. Privacy International is a group of academics, writers, and lawyers directed by activist Simon Davies. Speaking about the awards to the press, Davies said that 'surveillance has now become an inbuilt component of every piece of information technology on the planet'. He hoped that the awards would be 'the beginning of a movement'. The awards were split into five categories and covered all forms of surveillance technology. The categories were corporation, local government, national government, product, and lifetime achievement.

The Lifetime Achievement Award was naturally won by the NSA's Menwith Hill listening station. The base commander of Menwith Hill declined the invitation to send a representative of the station to collect the award. Other awards went to Newham Council, in recognition of its pioneering use of surveillance cameras connected to face recognition computers that automatically identify 'people of interest'. A company called Harlequin won the

Product Award for its WatCall 'telephone traffic analysis system', which provides police with the ability to analyse who is phoning who. This allows the police to build 'friendship networks' of telephone users that can be linked into the Police National Computer to automatically identify 'people of interest' in a manner which they could not legally or efficiently do by other means.

Another award went to Esther Bull, a 19 year old student who discovered her landlord had installed a video camera behind a two way mirror in her flat. The lack of legal protection for personal privacy meant that she had to bring a prosecution under the 'bad landlord' law. The landlord had been taping her for over two years. This is precisely the sort of scenario that certain web site operators would exploit by connecting the video camera to the Web and charging people up to $10 per hour to spy on the woman over the Web. Not to mention the inevitable extra revenue generated by sales of video 'highlights'.

The Department of Trade and Industry was awarded for its farcical attitude to privacy and security of the Web – of which we shall be hearing more. A video was shown at the ceremony of a Privacy International activist being dragged from the DTI by several burly police officers after he had tried to present the award.

Governments around the world are at present reluctant to relinquish their interest in using the Web for surveillance. As we shall see in later chapters, the technology to secure the Web through encryption is already available. Governments, however, are trying to outlaw such technology, offering inferior alternatives that the industry and the public alike have dismissed. The current situation for privacy on the Web is confused, and the confusion is exploited by all manner of individuals and organisations, eager to profit from infringements of privacy. It is a situation that has caused mistrust among consumers, and is preventing the Web from attaining its full commercial potential.

Net Spies

YOU HAVE MAIL

One of the most common privacy invasions is the collection and trade in user's email addresses. Unlike Tom Hanks and Meg Ryan most users' mailboxes are not filled with endearing declarations of love, but instead are swamped with adverts – known (for obscure reasons) as SPAM. Everything is offered; overpriced telephone sex chatlines, instant 'fast-cash' scams, and, of course, mammoth lists of email addresses are for sale. The email systems are being all but overwhelmed by electronic junk mail but there is little than can be done to keep email addresses private.

Telephone subscribers have the option to specify an unlisted number, but no such option exists with email addresses. No effort is spared in the collection, and compilation, of vast mailing lists of email addresses. Almost as soon as a new mailbox or mail address is used, it begins receiving all manner of solicitations, many of which are nothing more than attempts to swindle the mailbox owner. As much as 30 per cent of all email is unsolicited. For a long time, the sending of such unsolicited commercial email (UCE) has been regarded as an invasion of privacy. UCE – known on the Web as 'spam' – is similar in nature to telemarketing, which is also widely regarded as intrusive. With email, though, it is cheap and easy to send mailshots to literally millions of users. Spam has become such a popular marketing method that there is a thriving trade in lists of email addresses. These lists are produced by harvesting email addresses from the Web – many of them are obtained, and sold, without the owner's permission.

Most email users quickly become irritated and offended by the sheer quantity of spam they receive, and as a result laws are being enacted in a bid to prevent it. The majority of this kind of email falls into two broad categories; adverts for sex sites, and ill-disguised swindles.

Legitimate companies, particularly if they have a presence on the Web, will not send spam. Those that have done so in the past quickly found that their networks became unusable when millions of users replied by email to complain. In some cases people have used the Web to organise email protests against such companies. These protests have taken the form of millions of users simultaneously sending email to the offending company in an effort to overload– and crash– the company's network.

Many Internet service providers will not allow their users to send mass email, and will revoke the accounts of those guilty of such antisocial behaviour. This does not solve the problem, because it is so easy for senders to hide their real identity, partly because of unscrupulous web sites. The source of much spam is from the 'free trial' internet accounts. Spammers will sign up for a month, send a couple of million junk mails and then move on to another free account, under another name, even before the service provider can ban them from the system. These conditions have made email an ideal new avenue for exploiting age-old scams, scams that are illegal if sent by regular mail.

Pranksters, also, have discovered an amusing new pastime creating hoaxes that will generate incessant email. An unknown, but not small, proportion of all the email sent consists of such content that is often illegal, and serves only to clog the system and waste people's time. Unfortunately people, particularly new users, continue to reply to these adverts, frequently losing money in the process. Unlike junk mail coming through the post, spam email costs the recipient money to collect.

Research by the US government suggests that in the US alone, email users are being 'ripped-off to the tune of billions of dollars'. Those are the very words of the Federal Trade Commission. The sending of spam generates cash for the senders. When they send out ten million copies of a new scam it is almost certain that someone, somewhere will be fool enough to part with cash, on the off-chance that promises made will come through and it can be difficult to trace the persons responsible.

Most of the adverts sent by email are true 'junk mail'. Examples of the most common spam 'advertisements' include: invitations to join get-rich-quick schemes (suitable only for the most reckless investors); adverts for 'free' sex sites, which are often sites acting as covers for credit card fraud operations. There are also pleas for charitable donations – for charities neither you, nor anyone you know, has never heard of; unoriginal hi-tech variants of ancient chain mail and pyramid selling schemes and hoax virus alerts.

Some of the hoaxes can be amusing, such as the fake press release 'Microsoft Corporation Buys Vatican' released on April 1st. Others are designed to cause problems. A favourite and recurring hoax, that causes much annoyance to system administrators, is the 'Good Times Virus' alert. This is a message that is circulated to groups of users warning them of a virus that spreads by email that typically will erase all the data on users hard disks, or do other unspeakable horrors to your data. Users are encouraged to pass on the message to others. Many users do pass on the message, and many more bombard the system administrator with worried queries about non-existent viruses.

This hoax is similar to a chain letter where the original writer is trying to send a message that will circulate forever.

Another such hoax, which plays upon people's sympathies, is the 'DyingLittle Boy' message. This hoax relates the sad tale of the terminally ill boy whose dying wish is to get into the Guinness Book of Records for receiving the most email messages. Everyone is encouraged to reply to the address given, and then pass the message on to their friends.

This type of hoax, and its variants, is usually constructed to cause the given email address to become flooded with thousands of messages of misplaced sympathy. Unlike mainstream chain letters, in which someone is trying to make money and must run the risk of being traced, hoaxers are almost impossible to trace. A chain of hoax mail can be started by sending one well-targeted message to people that are most likely to pass it on. University and college email networks are particularly prone to these hoaxes.

Commercial chain mail, on the other hand, has existed for almost as long as the postal system. The general theme of chain mail is the same. A list of, say, five addresses are sent out to many people.

Recipients are told to send a small amount of money to each of the five names, replace one of the addresses with their own, and send the revised message on to as many people as possible. The promise is that their name will end up on thousands of copies of the mail and they will receive thousands of small cash gifts. Schemes such as this are almost always illegal and most people who participate lose money.

The Web, with its easily obtainable lists of email addresses, is perfect for those exploiting chain mail. It can be difficult to trace the operators of such schemes, and even if they are traced they may be in a foreign country, making prosecution difficult if not impossible.

Other scams involve 'miracle' products, aimed at one's self esteem.

Cures for baldness; instant weight loss; effortless income, and 'ancient recipes' for preventing impotence. All are offered by email and, if ordered, the majority of them not surprisingly fail to work (if they ever arrive). Solicitations for products like these are often part of an illegal pyramid selling scheme. These schemes tell of how the 'exclusive product' cannot fail to sell. You are encouraged to buy bulk and sell through your own 'distribution network'. Pyramid schemes such as these only ever make any money for the people at the top of the pyramid and they quickly collapse, causing most people to lose money.

Investment 'opportunities' are also frequently offered online. These are usually supported by testimonials from existing investors. This type of scam is known as a Ponzi scheme, in which the early investors are paid not out of profits but out of the money provided by later investors. Ponzi schemes also quickly collapse; as soon as no new investors can be found and there is no money coming in to meet the payments. Promoters of Ponzi frauds will usually operate a particular scheme for a short time, collect the money, and close down before they can be detected.

The Web is again, ideal for this type of fraud. Adverts for sex sites are probably the most common examples of spam. It is virtually impossible to avoid receiving unsolicited invitations, and one need not have visited a sex-related site to receive the spam.

Mainstream sex sites are operated by large, and usually well known, organisations and they do not need to resort to mass email campaigns to market their services. Successful and legitimate concerns are able to afford the more usual forms of advertising, such as banner advertisements on other sites. However, there are many sex sites that make their money not from legitimate popularity, but by exploiting visitors' reluctance to formally complain that they have been overcharged for porn. Such sites claim to be 'free' for members but they require their visitors to supply their credit card details in order to join.

Membership itself is free, but a valid credit card is cited as necessary for proof of age. Once these formalities are complete, members are issued a username and password, (to protect children of course) and they are finally granted access to the 'free area', probably unaware of charges to come.

Members are bound to the terms and conditions of the membership agreement. A file containing that agreement is most likely lurking somewhere in the nether regions of the web site in desperately small type, included only because of legal requirement. A condition of the agreement will usually be along the lines of 'all accesses to material outside of the"Free Area"', (normally almost everything on the site) 'will be charged to the credit card supplied as part of the agreement'.

Promoters of such sites are usually acting within the laws of the state or country in which they are operating, and as a result, there is little that people can do to recover any unexpected charges made. Credit card companies, and their refund departments are unlikely to be sympathetic towards cardholders' claims based upon the cardholders' failure to read the contract. They are even less likely to accept liability for such reckless use of a credit card and may even draw the cardholders' attention to their own fine print. They would give age-old advice that always applies when entering into any sort of financial agreement: 'Think carefully before you sign'.

Adult-oriented web sites are very much a case of caveat emptor, and people that feel they've been overcharged frequently accept culpability, not least because of the embarrassment involved in speaking out. Such activities are not necessarily breaking any laws, so these sites are making a lot of money. The way these sites make their money, however, tends to rule out the possibility of attracting much in the way of repeat business. Such sites rely on a constant stream of new visitors to ensure their profitability. To attract such a stream of visitors they must market themselves aggressively. Since they do not offer value for money they would cease to make any if their name became well known. They need to change their name and appearance fairly regularly to keep the visitors coming – although the content remains a constant. And the Web is ideal for this; the schemes can operate for an extended time and the various web pages used can have a very professional appearance.

However, the methods they use to invite new visitors are less than professional: sending mass email is a popular method. With modern email systems, the site promoters invite millions of people to sample the 'free' site by simply clicking on the address given. Clicking on this link will start up the web browser and connect to the web site to be given the hard sell. The sales pitch usually contains material unsuitable for viewing by children. Parents who wish to allow their children to use email should take precautions to filter and vet their children's email. It is also advisable for parents to set up their children's web browsers to block any access to potentially harmful sites.

This is a particularly important precaution because of another method of promotion used by these sites. Sex-related sites and other direct marketing sites will intercept a user's web browsing session.

This is no exaggeration; many web browsing sessions are all but hijacked by web pages that use advanced features of the Web, to redirect people's browsers to another site. The promoters of sex sites will pay to attract visitors, and they pay other web page owners to place a link to their sex site on the page. The payment is generally only a few cents for every person who uses that link to visit the sex site.

The web site uses its log files to find out the previous page that each new arrival was using, and in that way, the advertiser can find out which link was followed. The owner of the web site, which passed the visitor on is then paid on a monthly basis.

In itself, this appears to be a perfectly normal – and acceptable form – of advertising. The Web, far from being normal allows quick profits to be made from this type of advertising. Normal advertising allows the consumer the choice whether or not to request further information. This type of 'commission-paying link' advertising can be configured to remove that choice from consumers, by interrupting browsers and forcing passers-by onto the sex site sales area.

Sometimes, endless loops of pop-up adverts can make a person's web browser unusable, leaving no choice but to shut them down – which in itself can be difficult as pop-ups may appear as fast as they can be closed. Each time a user's browsing session is successfully redirected to the sex site, a commission is paid. People can, and have earned thousands of pounds by running such web sites that exist solely to earn commission from the advertising links they contain, often providing no information content of their own other than adverts.

Advertisers are able to do this by constructing web pages which contain hidden programs and instructions to the browser. These can produce a pop-up window linking to any site, or alternatively they can redirect the main browser. To encourage people to visit such pages, the owners will often falsely describe them in search engines, or place them on pages along with certain types of popular material of dubious legality.

Bootlegged audio files are available for download from the Web, offering almost CD quality music. The same fate befalls software, and there is a large underground network of sites distributing copyright infringed material. Offers of free software, or free CDs, will often encourage people to visit the site. The only way to avoid this kind of browser hijacking is to disable the browser's advanced features, and hence lose much of the Web's functionality. Not content with merely invading mailboxes and taking control of web browsers, many of these sites also pollute search service databses with spurious links. Many web pages are programmed to earn commission by redirecting visitors to pay sites have a particular feature in common.

There may be a large, and apparently blank area, usually at the bottom of the web page. It is, however, anything but blank; there is in fact a large file there, containing invisible black text against a black background. This text is typically the entire contents of the English dictionary. It tends to be hidden from view to prevent visitors wondering why the page has a dictionary embedded within it which seems to serve no purpose other than to delay the time it takes the page to load. But the reason why these sites include a dictionary is to ensure that when it is copied into a search database it will be selected as a match for almost any word or phrase in the English language.

This causes a major problem for the maintainers of search services, as their databases quickly become filled with multiple copies of the dictionary. It also causes poor performance of the service; and users who are confronted with endless lists of adverts for sex sites quickly tire of using the service. Database maintainers will delete items that abuse their service in this manner, and they may even blacklist certain sites. The search engines themselves are becoming sophisticated enough to discriminate against such abuses. But the ease with which these advertisers can change to another site and submit them into the databases again is a constant problem for search data-bases, and one that is largely unavoidable for users.

The hijacking of web browsers and the pollution of search databases are relatively easy for users to avoid, compared to combating unsolicited commercial email. It is a problem that affects most people on the Web and has proved almost impossible to wipe out. It persists because it is effective, and because of the ease with which email addresses can be collected and compiled into vast mail-ing lists. Many commercial sites now routinely require new visitors to identify themselves to the system. Typically access is denied until the visitor fills in a short questionnaire and enters their email address. Other sites collect email addresses in ways that are more subtle, offering, for example, to notify visitors whenever the page is updated. A useful service for which they naturally require your email address. Some sites are just downright dishonest, containing hidden programs that will try to obtain your email address from your browser without your knowledge.

Many of the sites that ask for your email address usual-ly contain a checkbox where you can specify that your address is not to be divulged. On most European web sites this is a legal requirement of data gathering. In other places, such as the US, it is purely a voluntary offering which need not be adhered to. Even the giant computer corporation Sun Microsystems, who themselves maintain a large and innovative presence on the Web, has recently been accused of sharing email addresses after being instructed not to.

Dave English, a consultant engineer from New Hampshire, had cause to visit Sun's web site. Before he could gain access to the information he was seeking, he had to complete a small survey and give information about his occupation and contact details. Instead of entering his own email address, English created a dummy account –what direct marketers call a 'decoy' – and gave that email address to Sun. English never used the account but shortly afterwards it began to receive email solicitations from companies that were business partners with Sun.

Sun Microsystems are a member of the Online Privacy Alliance (OPA), a body that opposes the introduction of privacy laws and campaigns, instead, for self-regulation. The OPA claim that self-regulation is the best way to protect consumer privacy. On their opening web page they invite visitors to join the OPA. Naturally they require them to give the following information: who they are, where they live, email address, telephone, and fax number. And why not? They may need to be able to contact members in emergency situations. To warn them about impending privacy rights violations, perhaps? They also offer to inform visitors whenever the site has been updated; simply give them your email address.

'The Online Privacy Alliance', the web site says, 'is a diverse group of more than 60 global corporations and associations who have come together to introduce and promote business-wide actions that create an environment of trust and foster the protection of individuals' privacy online.' Their opposition to privacy laws isn't even mentioned in this, their welcoming message. That elusive 'environment of trust' is almost immediately put to its sternest test when in paragraph two of the welcome message, visitors are invited to 'simply fill out the form below'. Visitors are reminded, however, that it is the site's policy not to divulge information and it displays a prominent, albeit brief, privacy policy.

The privacy policy fails to make clear whether or not your personal data is distributed among the 'more than 60 global corporations and associations' that form the

OPA. You can be certain your details will not get sent to any of their competitors who are not members of the OPA.

In the absence of legally binding privacy policy it is possible for organisations to profit from exploiting personal data. There are many examples of sites on the Web that appear to offer something for free. An 'email address for life' perhaps, or some free web pages. These sites will require users to give personal information before they can make use of the 'free' facilities on offer.

One such company, Hotmail, provides free email addresses via the Web. It pays for this service out of the funds it receives by hosting advertisements on the web pages its users access their mail through.

When a user follows an advertising link, Hotmail sends their personal details to the advertiser. Another such company, Geocities, provides free web pages. In August 1998, Geocities' stock price plunged after the Federal Trade Commission punished them for deceptive trade practices when they were found to be violating their own privacy policy.

There are software packages available that attempt to prevent such email and scam web sites from being inadvertently viewed. Mostly, however, these are either inadequate, or they rely upon the co-operation of offending web sites. Most of these have to be configured by the user and are aimed primarily at making the Web more suitable for children. They can automatically censor out adult oriented sites and bad language.

In many cases such software is adapted by the service provider to further invade privacy by vetting and censoring the content of user's communications. Keyword searches are performed on email and many sites become inaccessible at the service providers discretion.

Some of the more expensive products are aimed primarily at business users who wish to cut down on employee time-wasting. Typically these attempt to block employee access to sex sites by, for example, preventing any web page that contains flesh tones or words like 'fuck' from being viewed.

These packages probably do not provide the performance of the kind of software in use at Menwith Hill, but they do give an indication of the techniques in use. The products attempt to prevent users from viewing, or sending, messages containing content that the network owner does not allow, or does not approve of.

This software can maintain a 'blacklist' of addresses from which it will not accept emails. Netcom and America On Line (AOL) are two of the most heavily blacklisted email providers – possibly because their 'Free Trial' periods are often abused by people who just want a temporary account to send spam from. Alternatively, the software allows a company's email administrator to specify a 'white-list' containing only those email providers (such as business partners and clients) from which email is accepted, and reject all other email.

Keyword searches can also be used to reject any mail that is not for business purposes, mail containing illegal or offensive content, or mail of a personal nature, according to the wishes of the email administrator. Keyword searches are, however, a very hit-or-miss practice. For example, in 1996, AOL attempted to improve its image by installing software that automatically prevented its users from sending messages that contained any of a specified list of 'vulgar' words. It seemed strange that an American corporation would restrict free speech in such a manner, and it descended into a farce when a British user living in Scunthorpe was barred by AOL from sending his address because his town name contained a 'vulgar' word. Automated censorship software will inevitably make such errors, since it cannot have the intelligence to understand the context of human language. AOL now employs staff to vet user's messages. Staff are alerted to potential vulgarities by the software, and it is the staff that must judge whether to allow the message to pass, whether to officially warn the vulgar user, or whether to seek a decision from a higher authority.

AOL provides its staff with guidelines on what should be censored. Pick of the bunch is their attempt at the monumentally difficult, and still largely unresolved, problem of defining vulgarity itself. Their bizarre document 'Vulgarity Guidelines' makes for entertaining reading, as it contains what the AOL Censor considers to be 'examples of vulgar, conditionally vulgar, and acceptable phrases and subjects.'

Users of AOL are to be 'warned' whenever they use any of a long list of carefully defined vulgarities. For example, it is permissible for an AOL user to declare 'Virgins Wanted', but any message containing the words 'whips and chains', will automatically generate an official vulgarity warning.

Talking about sex is generally considered vulgar, but on the other hand, encouraging censorship of sex is specifically permitted: 'I didn't let my child see the movie because of the sex in it' is quoted in the guidelines as an acceptable use of the word 'sex'. The word 'suck' is in general considered to be vulgar, however the guidelines stress the following important exception. 'A member may say that AOL [...] sucks.'

And well they might, because the paragraph following directly after this exception explains to staff that AOL 'do not want to appear to censor members who speak out against us.'

Not all providers will censor their user's content in such a way. In any case, it can often be self-defeating; Users sometimes attack such censorship by attaching the very list of banned words to every message they send, thus overwhelming the censorship system by making it take action for every message. The human operators will then spend hours of their time deleting the same list from each message, before they can decide whether its actual content is vulgar.

Many providers do not attempt any form of censorship, maintaining (such as Demon Internet Ltd.) that they are simply the carriers of user data and are not responsible for the content of user items. Most service provider agreements require users to give a clear warning to people about possibly offensive content. Such rules and practices did not, however, prevent the fictitious Fulchester Underwater Canoeing Klub from registering their acronym as an official Internet domain.

Censoring the communications of Web users by using keyword searches has become increasingly common, ostensibly to help service providers 'clean up the Web'. Similar software is also used by corporations to monitor the content of messages that their staff send over the Web. In this case though, the keywords will be specially designed to prevent employees from revealing trade secrets. Censorship of web browsing is also used by companies, mainly to prevent their staff from downloading material with an illegal content, for which the company could be liable.

One of the programs on the market offers administrators the option to censor any Web page that features pictures containing 'fleshtones'.

Most ISPs take steps to prevent their networks from being used to send spam, and some try to prevent spam from ever reaching their user's mailboxes.

So-called 'Spam Filters' can be set up but these are very much a 'stop gap' solution. They work by scanning for keywords but are unintelligent and may even end up filtering out legitimate mail. Filters may also be set to bar incoming email from certain notorious addresses that are often used by spammers. This is fine, so long as no one you want to speak to also uses those providers.

It is possible to install software that will scan all incoming email and filter out spam. For an ISP, this software has limited effectiveness, as it requires that the content of each email is analysed, which is a time-consuming and expensive process, and ISPs do not tend to have the resources of a NSA spy station. Realistically, ISPs are only able to filter out a relatively small proportion of spam, and most will slip through the net. If these filtering systems are to work to their optimum capability, they will require the co-operation of the sender, but if the mass email is being sent for fraudulent purposes, it is highly unlikely that the sender will offer his or her assistance in getting the mail deleted. After all, the easiest way for a spammer to co-operate is simply not to send us their rubbish in the first place.

Senders of bulk email will go to any lengths to hide their identities. They will often sign up for 'free trial"'Internet accounts and use them to send as many emails as they can during the trial period – or until they are thrown off the system, whichever comes first. But sometimes, spammers steal the email identities of others and use them for sending spam mail, as American Jayne Hitchcock found out, when she began drawing attention to an organisation, or person behind an advert for what she believed to be a fraudulent service. The Woodside Literary Agency had placed an advert offering to represent writers but after sending in a proposal, Jayne was asked to pay a reading fee.

Alarm bells rang since the reading fees are prohibited activities for members of trade associations, so either Woodside was not a member of any professional or trade association or, if they were, they were in breach of the accepted code of conduct. A writer's discussion group on the Web secretly got involved in the Hitchcock affair and held an informal contest to see who could send the worst book proposal to Woodside.

All bar one of them (presumably the contest winner) were told their proposal was 'in the top 5% accepted by the agency'. All of them were then asked to send money to the agency. After a while, messages began to appear on the Web that appeared to have been sent by Jayne. The text of these messages, and the manner in which they were sent – forged sender's addresses and publicly displayed – was clearly designed to cause offence and elicit a massive response. These messages appeared to have been forged by Woodside in an attempt to flood Jayne's mailbox with complaints and thus silence her. In one of the forged messages, Jayne's home telephone number and address (known to Woodside from the original proposal) were posted publicly on the Web and the message claimed that she was 'interested in sado-masochistic fantasies.' She was also 'mailbombed' – a process where large volumes of email are sent to one address to render it unusable. The mailbombing extended to her husband, her agent, and her employers. Her name, addresses, and telephone number were placed on racist sites and sex sites, inviting people to call her or come to her home anytime 'day or night'. Clearly, she had been upsetting someone.

After setting up a legal fund, Jayne Hitchcock filed an aggravated harassment suit against the Woodside Literary Agency and its owners.

The NY Attorney General's office also filed a suit against Woodside Literary Agency et al for false advertising, deceptive business practices, fraud and harassment. Jayne also testified at the Maryland State House in support of a bill to outlaw email harassment. Partly due to Ms Hitchcock's two year campaign, it is now illegal in Maryland to 'use electronic mail for a communication made with intent to harass one or more persons or by sending lewd, lascivious or obscene material.'

New anti-spam laws being introduced in the United States will require all unsolicited commercial email to contain the name, address, email address and phone number of the sender. Direct marketers will also be required to comply with recipients' requests to be removed from mailing lists. Quite often, spam messages will advise users to 'reply with the word REMOVE to be removed from the mailing list'. Users who did just that were often removed from the mailing list, only to have their email address added to other, more valuable, lists containing only email addresses known to be active. These lists are more valuable because it is known that the messages are going to an address that is in use. Many of the mailing lists in circulation use out-of-date or non-existent email addresses, and are clearly less valuable than refined lists. The market for email address lists is still thriving, and it remains to be seen whether laws to prevent it are enforceable.

The debate on spam, and what form the final legislation should take is divided into two camps, that of privacy vs. free speech, as are so many Web related issues. Privacy advocates view spam as a violation of their privacy rights and favour the banning of UCE.

Advocates of UCE claim for freedom of speech, saying that an outright ban goes too far in regulating Internet speech and commerce. Conflict between fundamental privacy rights and the constitutional right to free speech is a common feature of the online privacy debate in the United States. In Europe, on the other hand, there are new laws preventing the right to free speech from being abused by requiring the holders of computerised information, such as databases of email addresses, to keep the information private. The European laws are at odds with the United States' self-regulation approach, and they may also present a trade barrier or even, as some trade analysts warn, provoke a data war with heavy restrictions being placed on the international flows of data.

Net Spies

THE PAMELA ANDERSON PROBLEM

O ne of the first sectors of the market to grasp the commercial potential of the Web was the sex industry. One only needs to open any newspaper to read about how the Internet is infested with pornography, usually of the most shocking kind. There seems to be a new report out almost every day, which details the activities of paedophiles who use public communications networks to conduct their repulsive trade. Although many such reports are sensationalised, they are not entirely without foundation.

Anyone who surfs the Web without taking precautions to protect their identity can expect to find advertisements for sex sites in their mailboxes. Often these messages are themselves of an explicit and potentially offensive nature. There are also ways other than email, in which the sex industry uses the Internet to thrust itself upon the unwary.

In one way or another, the exchange of sexual favours for money has been with us ever since trade began. Sex is, and always has been, a major seller and is used by advertisers to solicit the purchase of everything from motor cars to margarine. The selling of sex itself is a major business in its own right, although it is frowned upon in most countries, and illegal in many.

In countries such as the UK, where trade in pornography is outlawed, production and imports are heavily policed. Traditionally, checks were carried out on photographic materials, but nowadays video tape and computer disks also need to be searched. A Customs officer at Heathrow, who does not wish to be named, says that the memories of laptop computers are now routinely inspected for pornographic material entering the UK and they are apprehending a growing number of offenders.

According to journalist Simon Davies, the files on laptop computers are not only inspected as a matter of routine but copies of all the files – including deleted files – are kept by customs officials to be inspected at leisure. Customs and Excise regard the contents of computer memories and disks as no different to the content of suitcases. Customs require neither authorisation nor grounds for suspicion to inspect the contents of luggage and, in the absence of Home Office guidelines, they are content to apply this line of reasoning to electronic data. Civil liberties groups may feel that the inspection and subsequent return of luggage is, however, radically less intrusive than the taking and keeping of a complete copy of a computer's contents – including personal mail, financial records, and proprietary business information. How many innocent travellers would be content if on entering the UK their diaries and business papers were routinely photocopied by Customs officials?

There is a big difference between inspection and copying, which can be thought of as a form of seizure. Chris Sundt,chairperson of the Confederation of British Industry's Information Security Panel, takes a similar view; he has been calling for the establishment of Home Office guidelines to ensure adequate protection of security and personal privacy. The Customs & Excise press office spokesperson, Ms Alex Strutt, was willing to confirm that Customs officers have been copying the contents of laptop computers. She says that laptop computers being brought into the UK were searched for a trial period only. The trial was stopped in late 1998 and the contents of laptop computers are no longer being subjected to random 'stop and search' procedures. The reason for the trial was, said Strutt, 'basically, laptops are used to smuggle child porn images.' When asked if any successful prosecutions had resulted from the searches she said at first that she didn't know, but later added, 'Basically we are evaluating the results of the trial'.

This method of search is not unfamiliar. 'Keyword searches were performed,' according to Strutt, '[looking] for anything of interest to Customs & Excise.' Of course she would not add any details about what Customs & Excise may be interested in, apart from illegal pornography. 'Uninteresting data,' she added, 'has been destroyed'.

There are several problems here. The first is that using laptop computers is not the only way of smuggling computer porn into the UK. A far easier and more efficient method is to download it from the Web over a telephone line. Are Customs & Excise also monitoring the Web for child porn smuggled in such a manner? 'No,' said Strutt, 'it is not an offence to import images via the telephone network. This would be a police matter concerning possession.' Perhaps what she is referring to is the difficulties Customs would face in trying to monitor the telephone network. As such, they are content to leave it to other agencies more specialised in this area. As we have seen, someone is monitoring the telephone network in the UK, and it is unlikely that only the Americans are listening in.

A more serious question raised by the laptop 'seizures' is how a keyword search can be of use when one is searching for images. Images do not usually contain many words. Ms Strutt would not comment on this, saying only that it was an investigative matter that could not be revealed. She also declined to comment on what software package was being used to perform the keyword search. 'That,' she said, 'is a confidential matter between Customs & Excise and our suppliers.'

The implication is that Customs officers are using sophisticated keyword search software purchased from a specialist supplier. If they are performing keyword searching for images, what are they really looking for? The only 'words' one would expect to be connected to image files would be the name of the file itself. A search could be made of all filenames on a computer – including deleted files – looking for filenames indicative of images. However, this sort of search facility is a standard feature of all laptop computers and it does not need any extra software. Customs could, on the other hand, be using software that examines images to look for suspected porn – software, for example, that analyses the colour content of images and brings those containing 'fleshtones' to the attention of investigators. This does not, however, constitute a 'keyword search'.

Keyword searches are used for one thing: to examine the words contained in text documents (such as email). Keyword searches do not and cannot examine the contents of image files. So what were Customs really looking for? Was it, as their Press Office states 'child porn images'? Or was that just an excuse to cover up their true interest: economic and social intelligence gathering from the documents laptop owners keep on their computers? The statements made by Ms Strutt just do not add up and the readers must draw their own conclusions. Readers are also advised not to carry any private information on laptop computers, especially when crossing in and out of the UK, just to be on the safe side.

In the years following their introduction, the sale of new items of technology such as video recorders and satellite television receivers were boosted by the easy access they gave to pornographic material. In Great Britain, the distribution of such material was thought to be covered by the Obscene Publications Act (1959) This legislation is very loosely-worded, so that it can be interpreted to include almost anything. It is so general that during the 1970s, the Oscar-winning children's cartoon, 'Tom and Jerry' was briefly banned in the UK after self-styled moral watchdog Mary Whitehouse's successful campaign that it was 'too violent'. When video recorders went on sale in Britain, and video rental shops sprang up in every town, it was soon discovered that the OPA did not apply to material stored on magnetic tape. The law was amended and it is now loose enough to cover just about any material including, television, photographic, and electronic.

In the UK, the adage 'No sex please, we're British' still applies; erotica is widely considered to be immoral, offensive and even a danger to the community. Britain is out of step with its European partners on this issue, in that in most other EU countries hard-core pornography is freely available, being regarded (for the most part) as harmless fun. Indeed, in some countries of the Union, hard-core porn is available on Pay-TV and there are many television stations in Europe that broadcast material that is legal locally but is considered offensive elsewhere. When television satellites are used for such broadcasts, they tend to cover a wider area, generally the whole of Western Europe. The situation is almost at the stage where explicit Scandinavian pornography is being broadcast into the unwitting homes of shocked British viewers.

There is good news, however, for the sensitive viewer, or for those who fear their children may lose their innocence by being exposed to sex at too young an age. All of these broadcasts are encrypted. They may only be received and viewed with a special decoder and these decoders are not officially for sale in the UK. It was thought for a while that the banning of sales could contravene the Treaty of Rome. Technically the terms of the Treaty do not allow trade restrictions to be imposed between member states, but there are many 'opt-outs'. Fearful of the reaction of the British electorate to an invasion of 'Euro-porn', the Conservative government of the day negotiated just such an opt-out to cover offensive material. This did not, however, prevent the sale of 'home-made' decoder equipment, and now the satellite TV magazines are full of advertisements for 'pirate decoders'. The Web is another way in which national policy on offensive material can be circumvented. The quantity of potentially offensive material that is available on the Web is often difficult to avoid. Web sites specialising in pornographic material are among the most heavily visited on the Web.

Millions of adverts for 'adult' or 'XXX rated' web sites are sent by email every day. Most users of the Web regularly receive such email even though they have never visited any of these sites, and indeed may never intend to visit such pages. Site operators know that mass email is a cheap and effective way to generate revenue – and some of these web sites are making vast sums of money. The fact that some children are receiving their explicit material, suitable only for adults, does not appear to deter them from using such methods.

Many adult web sites are legitimate concerns, but many are not. Some are little more than a cover for a swindle operation that relies on the reluctance of victims to admit having been swindled while they were trying to buy pornography. For example, many sites will claim that they wish to protect minors. To do so, they insist that people can only access the adult areas of their site after they have provided proof of age. How do people prove that they are adults over the Web? Simple. They give the web site their credit card details. Once verified, they may freely access the site's content. Not a good idea; almost everything viewed on the web site will be charged to the credit card, as per the terms of the easily overlooked small print.

Another porn-related Web scam was discovered in Canada, where there is a thriving sex industry. It was there that a man exposed a swindle after being defrauded out of several thousand Canadian dollars. He had visited an adult site on the Web that required him to download and install software before he could access the site's content. He did so and was then able to participate in an interactive video strip show.

It wasn't until his telephone bill arrived that he discovered just what the software installed had done. The software could only be used while he was connected, and online via the telephone to the Web; the software had been cutting his connection to the Web and reconnecting him via an expensive premium toll service. This toll service was based in the Ukraine. One can only imagine his surprise – and horror – when he saw the costly international call charges on his telephone bill. When the program was started, a message was displayed which claimed that it was connecting to the adult service, taking about 30 seconds. In the meantime, the software disconnected the phone connection, and turned the volume on the modem to its lowest setting and silently redialed the Ukrainian toll service to reconnect the user to the Web. As soon as reconnection was established the software would then display the adult content. The victim, who may go on to visit other sites, would be totally unaware that he or she were now paying premium rates. The site operator had hoped that his victims would be too embarrassed to report the fraud.

Other sex sites, particularly in California, are now providing cover for credit card fraud operations. Their purpose is to collect credit card numbers and establish small repeating charges on them, usually less than $20 per month, in the hope that they will go unnoticed. The Web makes it easy for such sites to be established quickly and to disappear equally fast. The operators of such frauds regularly change the addresses and names of their web sites so that the fraud remains undetected. Other sites specialise in voyeurism, and these provide some of the worst examples of privacy violations.

Canadian actress Pamela Anderson and her then husband Tommy Lee discovered that there are other ways in which the Web pornography trade can infringe a person's privacy. While on honeymoon, Pamela and Tommy made an explicit home video for their personal use. At that time Pamela Anderson was the star of the successful television series Baywatch, in which scantily clad men and women perform feats of heroics on the sun kissed beaches of Beverly Hills. Often nicknamed 'Babewatch', the physical attributes of its cast have long been thought to be a major factor of its popularity. Unfortunately, the honeymoon videotape was stolen, according to the Lees, by a contractor working on their home in Malibu.

Shortly afterwards, the content of this video, which can only be described as hardcore porn, was being advertised for sale on sex sites all over the Internet. It had been converted into a form suitable for viewing on a standard personal computer and could even be viewed directly in web browsers. Thanks to the efforts of hackers and anonymous remailers, the video was soon made freely available on the Web. Video retailers obtained copies of the tape, either by downloading it from a public network or by other means, and have sold it on videotape for those who could not access the Internet.

Still images from the tape were published in Penthouse magazine's June 1996 edition. The Lees sued, claiming that Penthouse publisher Bob Guccione had invaded their privacy by publishing stolen pictures without the Lee's consent. US District Judge Stephan Wilson dismissed the lawsuit on several grounds, including the fact that they were both 'public figures', and that the theft of such a videotape was 'newsworthy'. Amazingly, part of the reasoning for allowing publication was based on Pamela Anderson previously having posed nude for Playboy magazine. This implies that under US Federal Law once someone has willingly posed nude, they forfeit any legal protection even of the most intimate secrets of their marriage. The court's decision, about which one has to struggle to avoid contempt, has allowed the entire video-tape to be openly sold.

The video is openly available, at least in countries where pornography is being openly sold. One retailer's advertisement reads: 'This is it! Available for the first time to the public, this is the legendary purloined honeymoon video of America's favorite tabloid couple. Stolen off of their bedroom table, the tape is an eye-opening look at the private moments of Pamela and Tommy before, during and after their romantic Mexican wedding [...] it's all here, from yachting to cooking to some down-and-dirty bedroom antics. What's gotten this video so much notori-ety is the sex, as two of the world's most famous folks bare it all for each other and their trusty camcorder. See for yourself Pamela's mouthwatering oral techniques...' And so it continues.

One can only imagine the deep embarrassment the general availability of such a video must have caused. However, sympathy for her plight might dissipate some-what, when one learns that early in 1998 a judge granted a temporary restrain order to prevent adult web site oper-ator, Internet Entertainment Group (IEG), from using their site to sell copies of a second Pamela Anderson sex video. In granting the order, US District Judge Dean Pregerson said release of the tape would violate their right to priva-cy.

Although the judgement does not condone people who profit from such privacy infringements, one might think that Pamela would have learned to be more careful with her more intimate mementoes. On the contrary, after her divorce from Tommy Lee, she entered into a relationship with another rock star. This time it was Poison singer Bret Michaels, and once again intimate videotape was made, mislaid, and destined for the Web. It was Michaels who applied for the restraining order pending a decision in his $90 million lawsuit against IEG. Michaels is alleging that the tape, in which he is dressed as a vampire with his 'private parts' exposed, will damage his career. On MTV News in January 1998, he was accused of 'being merce-nary' after 'he appeared on the Howard Stern show and', according to MTV, 'alluded to being willing to release the tape if the price was right'. Anderson has also filed a suit against IEG.

Some people, including IEG., have suggested that Michaels, and possibly Anderson, deliberately 'floated' the tape to attract publicity. The judge, however, did not find such evidence persuading. Judge Pregerson granted the injunction partially on the grounds that the Michaels-Lee claim of copyright infringement was sound. The court overruled, however, the 'fair use' exception of copyright law that allows small extracts to be freely reproduced. IEG's argument that they could publish a two-minute extract that had already been published on a Netherlands based site was also dismissed.

The court agreed with the plaintiffs that 'without their consent, a reproduction of their likenesses for commer-cial gain under any circumstances would be actionable, and the same went for a conventional privacy claim in that a couple's sexual encounter was an event that was presumptively private, intimate and not a matter of public concern, and whose dissemination would strike the aver-age person as "highly offensive".' Reasoning that is based upon the assumption under US law of an 'expectation of privacy'. However, Judge Stephen Wilson did not apply such reasoning in the case of the first videotape, which has become a best-seller on both video cassette and the Web.

In their defence, IEG cited Anderson's fame as a sex symbol and argued that because she 'has appeared nude in magazines, movies and', referring to the first tape with Lee, 'publicly distributed videotapes, the facts contained on the Tape depicting her having sex are no longer private'. This is arguably a naïve line of reasoning that suggests nudity and sex are the same thing, and it results in a blurring of the distinction between fiction and reality. I.E.G. also argued that distribution of the tape of Pamela engaging in sex with Tommy Lee negated her expectation of any future sexual relations she may have. The court was not prepared to conclude 'that public exposure of one sexual encounter forever removes a person's privacy interest in all subsequent and previous sexual encounters'.

The public interest generated by the glamorous lifestyles of the rich and famous has led many countries to consider the introduction of privacy laws. In general, however, such laws have been avoided on the grounds that they would violate the principle of a free press. A further argument against privacy laws is that they would only serve to protect the rich and famous, in whom the public is naturally interested, and would do nothing to protect the privacy of ordinary individuals. This is something that certain sex sites on the Web dramatically illustrate – those web sites that are dedicated to spying on the intimate behaviour of the public.

High-speed multimedia networks are beginning to replace the traditional binoculars of the Peeping Tom. The voyeur of the Nineties equips himself (they are usually men) with a functional network connection, and then prowls the Web in search of thrills. At first glance, it is difficult to imagine what kind of voyeuristic opportunities are available on a computer network. After all, computers do not have the sort of windows that can be peeped through, and neither do they contain any kind of keyhole that the aficiandos of peeping would consider viable. Multimedia web sites do, however, contain what some Toms may consider the next best thing.

There are a growing number of multimedia sex sites that offer live and recorded video feeds from strip clubs. Most, but not all, of these sites are available only by subscription and non-members are not permitted to enter or view the videos. Many of these sites are similar in nature to the kind of 'Peep Show' establishments that are found in Red Light Districts all over the world. In these places clients pay a fee to watch the erotic cavorting of naked models through a hole in the wall (thus the Tom's privacy is maintained). Many of these sites on the Web generate considerable revenue for their owners and there is intense competition between operators to attract customers. These sites are popular especially with inhabitants of states or nations where that kind of material is not obtainable, and more so because of the supposed privacy and ease of access afforded to clients who may not wish to be seen entering such an establishment in the street.

These sites use cutting-edge technology and techniques. They deliver live video feeds of strippers on demand to be viewed anywhere in the world in a web browser without the need for any special equipment or software. Considered from a purely technical perspective, the service offered by some of these sites is nothing less than an outstanding exploitation of the available technology. Just sitting passively and watching a strip show in a web browser is not the only thing on offer (although it is questionable as to whether the provider expects their customers to sit passively during the show!) There are also interactive shows where people may use the web browser to communicate with the performer – giving instructions, idle chit-chat, sex talk – whatever takes the client's fancy. In most cases, the conversations are typed into the web browser, but a growing number of sites are offering the ability for clients to use their existing multi-media attachments to talk directly with the models as if by telephone.

For decades, sci-fi movies have featured futuristic videophones in common usage in futuristic civilisations. Only recently have videophones started appearing, but they remain an expensive luxury of dubious quality used chiefly for videoconferencing within large corporations that can afford such extravagances. On the Web, however, this technology is available now for the cost of a standard PC and a local telephone call. But its main use so far is to contact strippers on the other side of the world.

But the seasoned Peeping Tom would consider stripping videos, interactive phone sex and real time colour motion pictures blasé. He would be on the lookout for something more; perhaps the thrill of obtaining an unintended glimpse of naked flesh. One may speculate endlessly about the motivations that drive Toms to Peep. A better insight may be gleaned, however, by examining the content of web sites dedicated to voyeurism. Many of these sites contain large archives of photographs of the rich and famous exposing themselves – either on screen or shot illicitly by the paparazzi. Many of the pictures available are referred to as 'Oops!' shots, recording for posterity the accidental exposure of a famous actress' nipple. The sort of humorous, tongue in cheek, pictures that have appeared for decades on the glossy pages of gossip magazines. Surely it is a harmless 'bit of fun' that causes no real embarrassment for the unfortunate victims. Other sites though are more disturbing, offering what are aptly named 'up skirt' files.

Such archives hold hundreds, or even thousands, of pictures obviously taken from a camera hidden at ground level and looking up. With a virtual nudge and a wink, viewers are invited to submit their own pictures with no questions asked as to how they were obtained.

A woman could, for example, be walking along the streets of New York, when her skirt is caught in an up draught and blows up over her head. She is not aware that she is in the field of vision of a hidden digital camera, strategically placed by a subway vent. With a smile she shrugs off the minor embarrassment, and continues on her way without giving the incident further thought. Within seconds, a photographic record of the event has been placed into an archive situated in California. Before the unfortunate lady can reach her destination (or indeed return home to change into a trouser suit), her picture could be available to hundreds of millions of people all around the world.

Although not impossible, the chance of these pictures ever being seen by someone able to identify her is slim indeed. However, should she learn that a picture of herself in her underwear is being distributed for commercial gain by a sex site on the Internet, statistical arguments are unlikely to mollify her.

She will become even more frustrated should she consider seeking legal redress, unless she is fortunate enough to have at her disposal better resources than the Anderson-Lees. It is safe to assume that the majority of the thousands of women who are having their personal privacy invaded in this way cannot afford to employ the legal talents of a Johnny Cochran.

The Pamela Anderson Problem

The next step on from 'up skirt' photographs, was the hidden camera. The first site to feature such material was the Playboy club in New York. Several cameras were placed in the models' dressing room. Cameras have been installed in bedrooms, showers, and even in lavatories. These are known as 'pee-cams', and as their name suggests, they capture one of the most private activities possible. There are now many pee-cams on the Web, and several sites specialise in them.

In the case of the Playboy site, there is no suggestion of privacy violation, since it is fairly obvious that the models knew about the 'hidden' cameras and were being paid to perform in front of them. The sites that are hiding cameras in public places, however, cannot make the same claim. A lot of sites feature the output of cameras hidden in showers, and many of them have the appearance of a set-up, where the person in the shower is paid to perform. With some, however, it is unclear whether the person being filmed is aware of the camera. One site, which was made available to the public by hackers, claimed that the two video feeds featured were from cameras which the site operator had secretly installed in the house next door to his. Cameras he had installed in the bedroom and bathroom of the person he pleasantly described as 'the slut next door'.

The worst example of privacy invasion must surely be a similarly hacked site that featured a novel variation on the pee-cam theme. This camera took a colour still photograph every few seconds and placed it on the Web. It also contained a large database of pictures it had taken previously. Like all pee-cams, the camera was hidden in a lavatory. Unlike other pee-cams, however, this one had been situated in the bowl of the lavatory. It is a considerable technical achievement to hide a camera in the bowl of a lavatory and broadcast its pictures around the world.

Presumably it was hidden inside a suitably modified dispenser of disinfectant, with the necessary wiring being hidden inside the rim and the plumbing. One has to wonder how many people would actually pay money to view the output of such a camera, but the existence of such material on at least one web site implies that there are people prepared to pay.

And what of the people featured (albeit from behind) in the pictures? Surely their privacy is being violated in the grossest manner. Unfortunately, the nature of the Web allows such sites to be located almost anywhere geographically. Anyone could be at risk of being exposed in such a way. The equipment needed to set up such a site and get it online requires no more than a laptop computer, a camera, and a mobile telephone. Such a site could be set up in minutes in almost any public lavatory, acquire thousands of pictures in a few hours, and be removed without a trace. Just about the only way this could be prevented is for law enforcement officers to install, and monitor their own CCTV systems in public toilets. It hardly seems any better, but vice and drug squad officers have been spying on lavatories for decades, and indeed CCTV cameras are being installed in some of the more notorious public toilets.

With toilet bowl pee-cams, it would seem as though we have hit rock bottom. Is there no human activity that cannot be made available to the world via the Web? Is this an invention that allows the world to look in on our most private acts? Such is the anarchic nature of the Web that the answer to these questions is an emphatic 'yes'. The darker side of the Web respects nothing and dismisses human dignity as though it was merely an instrument of repression. Even more shocking than the Peeping Tom sites are the growing number of web sites, masquerading in the guise of free speech, that are dedicated to images

The Pamela Anderson Problem

of death. These ghoulish sites collect from around the world photographs of scenes of crimes and accidents. They use sources as varied as news organisations, television, unscrupulous 'scene of crime' investigations, textbooks, and resources from the general public to compile archives of tasteless material.

Most of these sites are for paying members only, but others provide such material for free in what they laughingly consider a 'public service'. Scene of crime photographs of murdered rape victims are a particular favourite, as are the victims of shootings, road and air accidents and suicides. It is doubtful that the families of the victims would consider the worldwide distribution of such distressing images to be of service to the public. Amidst all these images of death and destruction, pictures of war deaths are strangely absent. Perhaps exposure to these images would cause dissent on the part of certain nations who may choose to express their foreign affairs policy with cruise missiles and other 'acceptable' weapons of not-quite mass-destruction.

It is these aspects of the Web that stretches the principle of free speech to its limits. Put to a vote, it is unlikely that a majority would mandate all of the above activities. It is possible that sites such as these will be the cause of a new international agreement and national laws that place restrictions on free expression. Laws that could all too easily be misused for purposes of political or social control. So far we have seen that the Web is an ideal medium for the activities of spooks, spammers, swindlers, and sexual exploitation. What we can do to protect ourselves against this, and to whom we can look to for assistance, will be the theme of the second part of this book.

Net Spies

HACKING THROUGH THE LEGAL JUNGLE

The Web has always been more or less self-policing, and any regulations that have been suggested are widely opposed. In any case, industry experts agree that any attempt to regulate the content of the Web on a purely national basis would be doomed to failure, because of the way in which the Web transcends national boundaries. However, at present each country is adopting its own approach to regulating the Web, and these regulations are often spurred on by hysterical Internet horror stories in the press. This unco-ordinated approach to regulating the Web is causing cross-border trade problems; for example, new privacy laws enacted in Europe make it illegal to export personal data to countries that do not have similar laws in place. In particular, the US is under pressure from Europe to protect personal privacy.

The legal status of online privacy differs widely between Europe and the United States. Since the 1970s, the European Union has been concerned with providing individuals with the legal means to defend their privacy, whereas the US government has always preferred to take a 'hands off' approach. In earlier chapters we have already seen examples of privacy breaches which have resulted from self-regulation. Problems of commercial exploitation and monitoring by governments generated calls from many Internet users to demand the means, legal or otherwise, to protect their privacy.

The member states of the European Union have enacted laws that require computer owners to ensure the privacy of any personal information stored on or processed with their computer. The Data Protection Act in the UK has been in existence for some years and it was amended in 1998 to bring it in line with European Law. However the US government continues to resist laws to enforce privacy, and it is trying to convince US trading partners to adopt a similar self-regulatory approach to online privacy. Europe and the US have reached a stale-mate over their opposing policies towards online privacy. Strangely both the EU and the US say that their own policy is necessary to promote electronic commerce. It is unlikely that they are both correct.

In October 1995, the European Parliament issued a 'data protection' directive for member states to introduce legislation for 'the protection of individuals with regard to the processing of personal data and on the free movement of such data.' The aim of the directive is to ensure that member states protect the rights and freedoms of consumers, 'in particular their right to processing of personal data'. Member states were required to enact suitable legislation by the end of 1998.

The Data Protection Directive requires that all personal data that is processed by computers in the EU be 'obtained and processed fairly and lawfully'. This means that personal information can be collected and used for a specified purpose and only with the permission of the person to whom the information pertains. The visible consequence of this is usually the small check box on a questionnaire that asks for permission to pass the information to other organisations. If permission is refused then the company collecting that information must not allow it to fall into the hands of any third party.

Personal data may only be 'stored for specified and legitimate purposes and not used in a way incompatible with those purposes,' and the data must be 'adequate, relevant and not excessive in relation to the purposes for which it is stored'. Organisations collecting personal information must inform the subject as to how that data is to be used. Companies processing personal data must also ensure that personal information on individuals is accurate. False data has to be removed. Another requirement that helps protect the privacy of individuals is that all personal data must, where possible, be stored in a manner that makes it impossible to identify the person it describes. Companies who wish to keep statistical data about its current customers for historical, or data warehousing, purposes must remove the person's identification from the data as soon as is practicable.

The Data Protection Directive also includes requirements governing the use of special categories of data such as 'data revealing racial origin, political opinions or religious or other beliefs, as well as personal data concerning health or sexual life'. The Directive requires that such data cannot lawfully 'be processed automatically unless domestic law provides appropriate safeguards'. A similar restriction governs personal data relating to criminal convictions. Security measures are also required to protect personal data against unauthorised access, alteration or dissemination. Additionally, companies storing personal data must take measures to protect their databases from the activities of hackers.

However, many of the sites on the Web are not taking these precautions, and moreover, if the web site is not based in the EU, it is not required by law to ensure these guidelines are upheld. As a result, vast amounts of personal data are being disclosed. A major problem is that no one is really sure as to what constitutes 'adequate security' of computer systems – short of locking them away or turning them off altogether. It will be difficult to comply fully with this aspect of the Directive, and so far, governmental reaction has been to predictably offer 'tougher sentences for hackers'. Although it is no easy task to keep computer systems safe from hackers, the protection of data on computers is not difficult, and this is the actual requirement of the Directive. Personal data can be encrypted cheaply and quickly in such a way that, even if hackers do obtain copies of personal data, they will not be able to read it. However, governments are not forwarding encryption as a solution, because it can also be used by the public to keep their conversations private and secret from the government. Installations such as Menwith Hill would be invalidated by encryption, as they would not be able to spy on the contents of encrypted messages.

The Directive also requires that individuals are able to inspect the data that is held on them. Everybody has the right to find out about the existence of any computerised file about them, and they are also entitled to know what the data is used for, along with the name and address of the organisation that controls the data. Having established the existence of such a file, people are entitled to inspect the file 'cheaply, and without delay'. There are certain exemptions to the above powers such as files relating to ongoing police investigations, which do not have to be divulged. There is also the exemption whereby secret files may be kept and processed for the catch-all purposes of 'national security'.

The self-regulation policy operating in the US follows similar lines but the major difference is that all such practices are purely voluntary. There is no requirement for any data-possessing organisation to follow the guidelines and no remedies are available to people who feel that their privacy has been violated. In a bid to make its policy more effective, the federal government in Washington DC has drawn up a code of conduct for the use of personal data. It has also promised to set up an Internet Privacy Watchdog but this has been subject to continual delay. The objective of the Watchdog will be to assess whether online companies use personal data properly.

The Privacy Watchdog, when it is set up, will be given the power to issue an electronic 'seal' to web sites that can demonstrate that they comply with a set of privacy principles. The privacy requirements that allow commercial web sites to display the seal are broadly in line with those set out in the EU Data Protection Directive. As there will be no legal remedy available to people who feel they have been wronged, companies must agree to work together with the Privacy Watchdog to resolve consumer grievances. Whether or not the Watchdog will be effective is in doubt. Even Russell Bodoff, the Chief Officer of the company that will run the Watchdog, has said 'there's no evidence I can give to you that American business in general is going to buy into this'.

The publisher of Privacy Times, Evan Hendricks, believes that the delays are a sign that self-regulation is unworkable. 'How much more evidence do we need?' he asks. The Federal Trade Commission director David Medine says that the FTC is holding back on judgement and may yet push for an online privacy law to be enacted. He first wants to see how many online companies actually adopt the privacy policies and the effectiveness of their remedies. The FTC gave the White House until the end of 1998 to get the scheme up and running. Privacy advocates also want progress. Deirdre Mulligan from the Center for Democracy and Technology hopes that 'a credible self-regulation scheme will fly. But,' she said, 'the White House has to continue to press industry to come up with an enforcement program with teeth'. As 1998 passed into 1999, the Privacy Watchdog was not up and running and President Clinton had other things, such as his trial for perjury, occupying his attention. Ironically, many of President Clinton's personal problems could have been avoided if only he had enacted Privacy legislation five years ago when he was first asked to.

The American attitude towards privacy is worrying European leaders, who have warned US companies that they may lose access to personal data held in the EU unless an effective means of protecting personal privacy is adopted. This is because of the section of the European Data Protection Directive relating to the transfer of data to non-EU countries. Any country that wishes to import personal data from the EU must comply with a minimum 'adequacy criteria' of privacy protection. It is illegal for data to be exported from the EU to countries that do not meet the adequacy criteria.

The Directive has been described as 'the most important international development in privacy protection for a decade' but concern has been expressed in the United States about the impact of the adequacy criteria. The Directive states that in determining the adequacy of the level of protection provided by a third country, account is to be taken of 'all the circumstances surrounding a data transfer operation [...] the nature of the data, the purpose or purposes and duration of the proposed processing operation'. The legal safeguards in force in the third country, and any professional rules or codes of conduct, are also to be taken into account.

The rules in place in the US at present, or rather the lack of rules, allow US web sites to make available unlisted personal telephone numbers from the UK. Anyone browsing the Web from Britain could find unlisted or ex-directory numbers on US web sites. This completely undermines the entire point of the British unlisted number service. The adequacy criteria of the Directive is designed to prevent the US web sites from obtaining the ex-directory numbers by making it an offence to export such personal information to countries that cannot ensure that it remains private.

Thomas Königshofen, Deutsche Telekom's Head of Section for Data Protection, describes the 'adequacy criteria problem' in some detail. In a recent speech he observed that 'talking about Issues in Privacy with respect to Internet Services is one of the biggest fields of regulation discussions in Europe.' Commenting on the Data Protection Directive he said it, 'has raised strong concerns – even with the US government – about the effects of this Directive on Transborder Data Flows and Global Electronic Commerce'.

Speaking about the chief danger of the incompatible US/EU approaches to personal privacy online he warns; 'This has been the motive for numerous negotiations between the European Commission and the US-Government to prevent a "Data Protection War" with harmful impacts for international business activities'. He gave figures indicating that over two thirds of Europeans are worried about how data may be gathered and used while they are online. He used these figures to justify the validity of the Data Protection Directive.

'The conclusions of the research,' he said, 'were that many Europeans are not willing to use Internet services if there is no control over the use of their private information.' He said the potential users were worried, 'by the fact that the personal information left behind might be used for other purposes, for example to sell to shops, without the prior consent of the user'. He also pointed to the majority support among Europeans that the EU should try to protect the personal information of its citizens.

Königshofen also gives the following example of an illegal act: 'If, for example, one realises that an Internet address, or IP number, is information that can identify a natural person [...] the collection or use of this IP Number for selling it to third parties is forbidden under European law.' Information attached to IP numbers is, as we have seen, routinely collected by web site operators. The owners of web sites in the US are not required to protect this information.

'The main concerns,' says Königshofen, are those rules governing 'the transfer of personal data to third countries.' Thus 'the transfer to a third country of personal data which are undergoing processing or are intended for processing after transfer may take place only if the third country in question ensures an "adequate level of protection". The adequacy of the level of protection afforded by a third country shall be assessed in the light of all the circumstances surrounding a data transfer operation or set of data transfer operations. Where the European Commission finds that a third country does not ensure an adequate level of protection Member States shall take measures necessary to prevent any transfer of data of the same type to the third country in question.'

'But,' he asks, 'what is an adequate level of data protection for the purposes of the EU Directive?' He gives five principles that are intended to specify the adequacy criteria. '1. The processing of data has to be fair. If it is to be fair, the data subject must normally be in a position to learn of the existence of a processing operation and must be given accurate and full information, bearing in mind the circumstances of the collection. Even more, any person must generally be able to exercise the right of access to data relating to him which are being processed, in order to verify in particular the accuracy of the data and the lawfulness of the processing.'

Secondly, 'the data must be adequate, relevant and not excessive in relation to the purposes for which they are processed. 3. The purposes must be explicit and legitimate and must be determined at the time of collection of the data. 4. The processing must be carried out with the consent of the data subject, unless there are lawful purposes, laid down in specific legal rules, which allow the processing of data without prior consent; and, last but not least, 5. An independent – internal or external

–Controlling Authority has to be appointed, which has the function and, moreover, the ability to ensure the internal application of these Data Processing Principles.'

As of the end of 1998, the United States has not met these adequacy criteria and there is uncertainty over the legality of allowing personal data to flow from the EU to the US. The European Commission has decided to postpone action to allow the United States to get its privacy act together. If, however, the US fails to put into place an effective Privacy Watchdog – or enact Privacy legislation – then it is likely that the European offices of American corporations will be unable to transfer personal data to their offices located in North America. For many global corporations, particularly those based in the US, this could prove to be an enormous obstacle to their activities and it would require massive reorganisation. The US would be sure to retaliate against Europe with trade restrictions of its own should this happen.

The Data Protection Directive is an example of legislation designed to protect consumers from intrusive sales and marketing techniques. There is a further aspect to online law that has the opposite intent. Many countries have adopted, or are planning to adopt, laws that intend to control the content of the Web and the behaviour of people when online. Unauthorised use of computers by hacking (or other means) is already a criminal offence in the United Kingdom and many other countries. Anti-hacking legislation outlaws anti-social acts such as deliberately breaking into and/or damaging computer systems or the data held on them. It is also an offence to incapacitate or compromise the performance of a computer by flooding it with, for example, a large amount of spam email, so that it cannot function for the sheer amount it has to process – a so-called 'Denial of Service' attack.

Another law being proposed by many countries, including the UK, is for the 'licensing of encryption services'. Encryption on the Web is a freely available technology that all but guarantees privacy on the Web. By licensing encryption services, the government perhaps hopes to retain its ability to spy on web users.

The legality of encryption is one of the most important issues relating to online privacy and it will be covered in the next chapter. What we shall concentrate on for the present is the activities of law enforcement agencies on the Web.

The traditional media – broadcasting, magazines, and newspapers – are all eager to sensationalise the Web and will pounce on almost any web-related news item. The old chestnuts of illegal and immoral shenanigans are an apparently abundant source of web-related scare stories. Hardly a day goes by without the press picking up some supposedly 'new' – but rarely exclusive – horror story from the Web. Child pornography is a favourite: in 1998 in the UK alone, there were over 200 separate reports about the multitude of paedophiles prowling the Web, using the wires to evade the justice they deserve.

If the reports in the press are to be believed, the Web must be chock-a-block with child porn and paedophiles. Such reports prey upon people's natural desire to protect children and such, they are sure to generate sales. Unfortunately, they also promote ignorance and misdirect the public's anger.

For all the reported incidents of child pornography on the Web very few of them have ever led to actual convictions. This is not because the Web is helping criminals to evade capture – most paedophiles are known to the police and are strictly monitored. Some well publicised investigations into alleged child porn have in fact proved not to involve underage material or illegal activity at all.

One such report was featured by Sky Television in August of 1998, in which they named an organisation that was 'distributing child pornography on the Web'. They reported the individuals concerned to the police. However, on investigation, it was found that the pictures were in fact images of adult models. Somebody, and no one knows who, used standard image editing software to replace the faces of the models with faces of children taken from such sources as holiday snaps. The Criminal Justice and Public Order Act makes it illegal to possess or produce photographs or electronically manipulated images which appear to be of children. It allows a maximum penalty of six months imprisonment. So, even though an illegal activity was reported, it was certainly not paedophilia.

The Web is being used to distribute child pornography but not to the extent some sections of the press would have us believe. There have been some successful investigations, often involving international co-operation. On the whole though there is very little child pornography on the Web, and what is there is not going to be easy to find by casual browsing. No Web service provider in their right mind is going to allow such material to be associated with their service. System administrators are vigilant for such abuses of their service and will not hesitate to take steps to prevent it. Any illegal material that is out there is generally confined to email.

Paedophiles have traditionally distributed photographic contraband through the surface mail. If they now choose to do so by email, little has changed and they may still be brought to justice. In most of the cases that have resulted in convictions, the paedophiles were using email as their method of distribution. The press frequently report, and sensationalise, almost any story mentioning children and obscene pictures, even when the pictures are not of minors, but they have to date remained silent on the subject of 'snuff videos' featuring children. An 'eye witness' video has been posted on the Web that shows in gory detail a young child being killed by a train. This has been copied onto many web sites, and is presented as a 'news' item. Some people have been exploiting the anger around child porn on the Web to exact revenge on those they have formed a grudge against. Posting anonymously, they can send illegal or offensive material to the person they dislike, or subscribe them to a mailing list that specialises in such material. Then, still posting anonymously, they will report that person to the service provider, or worse to the authorities. It is surprisingly easy for someone to hide their identity and use the Web to frame somebody in this manner.

As we have seen earlier, sex sites often give false information to web page search engines which causes unwanted pop-up browser windows displaying adverts for such sites to appear without warning. Unsolicited spam emails from the same sites often contain sample images. Both of these can cause unwanted files to end up on a person's computer. This would not be through any fault of their own, but it could be rather difficult to explain, especially to those people whose only knowledge of the Web has come from press reports.

This is the very problem that the seventies British pop-idol Gary Glitter (real name Paul Gadd) is currently facing. He was arrested in November 1997 after indecent images were allegedly found on his computer. He was charged with fifty offences under the 1978 Child Protection Act for allegedly possessing child pornography that police say was downloaded from the Web. The singer faces up to three years in prison if convicted.

Police were alerted by staff at the PC World store at Cribbs Causeway in Bristol. Glitter had taken his computer to the store to be repaired. Whilst repairing the computer, staff found the images. It is not yet clear why the staff were looking at files stored on the singer's computer, particularly since the contents of image files are unlikely to have any relevance to the repair of the PC. Were the PC World staff just being nosy, perhaps, or do they have some unspoken policy of inspecting personal data stored on computers given to them for repair?

A London solicitor who handles computer-related cases, Angus Hamilton, has suggested just that. Gary Glitter is not the only person to have been reported to the police by a high street chain store. Hamilton is handling a similar case that involves another computer taken for repair to PC World. In this case a man, to whom Hamilton refers as 'Simon', had taken his computer in for repair because the files needed to operate the stereo sound system on the PC were missing. This is a relatively straightforward repair job that simply involves identifying the make of sound hardware in the computer and copying the required files from a disk provided by the manufacturer (or downloaded from a web site). It should not take a professional more than thirty minutes to carry out – possibly less – and the hard disk on the computer does not need to be inspected.

But Simon's disk, like Gary Glitter's, was inspected. Staff claimed to be horrified when they allegedly discovered pictures of young boys on the computer. They called in the police. The files in question were stored on the hard disk in the area that web browsers use to keep a cache of recently viewed images.

Files can end up in the browser's cache for a variety of reasons: they may have been copied from web sites intentionally visited, or from sites that a person was tricked into visiting by a misleading link in a search engine or pop-up advertisement. It could even have been copied from an email sent to a discussion group or mailing list by a prankster.

A computer that has been used to log onto the Web may have hundreds, even thousands, of files stored on its hard drive that have been automatically copied from the Web. Often the owner is completely unaware that this has happened. Hamilton suggests that files copied in such a way are not really in the computer owner's possession, since he or she has no knowledge that they are there. If this were the case, people could not be prosecuted over the material that is put on their computer from the Web. The prosecution would have to show intent. This argument has not yet been established in law with respect to the Web, but it might provide a solution.

Simon's is a case in point. In mid 1997, he took his PC into his local PC World for repair. When the staff discovered the indecent picture files on his hard disk, they called the police, who arrested him on the spot. But Simon did not understand how the pictures of the boys came to be on his computer. He admitted that he had been browsing the Web and that out of curiosity, he had visited some of the more 'extreme' web sites. He denies deliberately downloading any such material. What many people do not realise is that the simple act of viewing information on the Web leads to it being stored on the hard drive of the computer that is online. Normally such files would be stored as a temporary internet file.

At the outset of the investigation, neither Simon nor the investigating officers were aware of the cache function of the browser software. Simon was prosecuted for possessing indecent photographs of children under the Criminal Justice Act, and was convicted in April 1998. This was in spite of the prosecution witnesses saying that it was impossible to tell whether the files had been deliberately downloaded or copied by the browser without

Simon's knowledge. He was placed on probation, lost his job as a teacher, and had to sign the Sex Offenders Register. In August 1998, Simon was cleared on appeal after the prosecution accepted that it was impossible to decide whether the files had been deliberately downloaded.

Of course, it is possible that Simon deliberately tried to hide illegal material by hiding it in the cache. This would however, require considerable knowledge of computer systems.

As Angus Hamilton comments, 'the prosecution in the lower court certainly seemed to have the "bit between their teeth" over the case and the feeding frenzy around the issue of paedophilia on the Net appeared to prevent them from objectively reflecting upon the technical matters in the case'. A further worrying aspect of the case was, 'both the prosecuting solicitor in the Magistrates Court and the three Magistrates trying the case were self-confessedly IT-phobic. The net result was that it was an uphill struggle to get them to see beyond the fact that pictures of little boys were on Simon's computer and to consider how they had actually got there.'

The Court of Appeal heard testimony from technical experts but as Simon himself comments, 'there did not seem to be anyone in that court room who thought that the conviction should stand.' Even though he was cleared of the charges, they are still disrupting Simon's life. As his solicitor says, 'Simon lost his teaching job as a result of the prosecution. Although it is now open to him to reapply for teaching posts, he is acutely aware of the likely impact of his having to explain that he has been out of work for over a year because he was wrongly prosecuted for possessing child pornography.'

Simon's name has been removed from the Sex Offenders Register and the Data Protection Directive should ensure that his name is removed from all electronic copies of the Register. In the United States things may have been a lot harder for Simon. Some US police forces are putting their equivalent of the Sex Offenders Register on the Web.

Thus, anyone in the world can visit the police web site and obtain the names, addresses, criminal records, and photographs of all registered sex offenders. There is also no Data Protection Directive in the US to ensure such sites are kept accurate and up to date. One of them recently, and incorrectly, listed a ten year old boy as a convicted sex offender.

Not only have the charges affected his career prospects, but the initial case generated considerable press coverage. And though quick to condemn, the press is rarely as keen to rectify errors or misjudgements. The press would do better to report on the real issues of online privacy and mass surveillance, for example, which receives little or no press coverage.

One wonders if perhaps the press feels that laws designed to protect personal privacy would restrict their freedom to report the news. Or perhaps they might even feel threatened by the Web because it is able to deliver news faster than the traditional print media.

The legal dilemma generated by the contents of cache directories is not an easy one to solve. If, on the one hand, the user is not to be held responsible for any data that has been automatically copied to their machine, knowledgeable offenders can easily exploit this.

Anyone wishing to evade such possession charges would simply keep all their illegal data in the web browser's cache and falsely claim that they didn't know it was there. Even technical details such as providing the date, the time the data was copied and the filename it was given can be forged to support their defence.

If, on the one hand, the user is not to be held account-able for any data that has been automatically copied to their machine this can easily be exploited by knowledge-able offenders. Anyone wishing to evade such possession charges could simply keep all of their illegal data in the web browser's cache and falsely claim that they 'didn't know it was there'.

It requires considerable technical knowledge to falsify the contents of a cache. It could be argued in court that the accused does not have the expertise and thus must be innocent. On the other hand, it only takes one unscrupulous expert to write and place on the Web a 'web cache falsifying' program. Then anyone could download the program and use the web cache to safely store illegal data of almost any nature. It would be very difficult to prove that the user was deliberately hiding the data.

There is little chance of a court judgement or legisla-tion being able to solve this problem. Each case would have to be taken on merit, necessitating, no doubt, lengthy technical arguments in each case. However, the Web's technology itself could solve this easily if the web browser was made to scramble everything it copied to a user's disk. All such files could be encrypted and authen-ticated in such a way that only the web browser can 'view' the content. It would then become a simple matter to prove whether the user of the browser had copied the suspect data.

The practice of keeping data encrypted would also help to ensure user privacy – few mass market producers are willing, however, to risk the repercussions of market-ing such data security. Although encryption is seen by many as the solution to the Web's privacy problems, and vital to the success of online trade it is not widely supported. Indeed, in some developed nations any use of secret codes is highly illegal. Strong encryption introduces a whole new set of problems with online crime. It is a powerful tool that offers many benefits, but like any powerful tool it can be misused. The fear amongst law makers and law enforcers is that strong encryption will make some crimes, very serious crimes, all but undetectable.

UNBREAKABLE CODES?

All forms of communication carry the risk of being overheard, but computer based systems are particularly vulnerable. With a little care, however, computers can be used to communicate with total secrecy. Encryption – the protection of information with secret codes – is a key solution available to protect data privacy and the materials on one's computer.

In fact, computers themselves were a direct development of research into encryption during the Second World War. A team of British mathematicians based at Bletchley Park had the task of breaking the secret codes that the German high command was using to communicate orders to its troops.

A mechanical device known as the 'Enigma machine' encoded the German's orders. Analysis of a captured Enigma machine revealed that there were millions of possible settings, but only one of them would correctly decode the German messages.

Alan Turing, mathematician and father of modern computing, finally cracked the code in 1941 by constructing the world's first computer, which was named 'Colussus'. This computer was able to eliminate many of the settings very quickly, and then try thousands of the other possible settings far quicker and more efficiently than a human operator could. The work at Bletchley Park was classified, and the existence of the Colussus computer remained a state secret until 1975.

During the intervening period, captured Enigma machines were donated by the British government to the governments of Commonwealth nations. These nations were told that Enigma machines were unbreakable, and would therefore provide secure communications. Colussus was then used to allow the British security services to spy on the private communications of its colonies and allies.

Net Spies

The Enigma Affair was a prophetic action of the government that foreshadowed the present-day anger and resentment caused by the impasse on encryption.

So, what is encryption? Quite simply, it is the act of encoding or scrambling a message, in such a way that a code of some sort is required to understand the original message.

One of the simplest secret codes, known to millions of children, is Caesar's Cipher. This code system dates back, as the name suggests, to ancient Rome. This code works by replacing the letters making up a message in a logical and consistent way. It is a type of 'substitution cipher' since it substitutes one letter for another. Caesar's Ciphers chooses replacement letters by shifting along the alphabet by a certain number of positions. For example, shifting letters one position in the alphabet causes 'a' to become 'b', 'b' to become 'c', and so on. So if the following message has been encrypted with Caesar's code 'EHZDUH WKH LGHV RI PDUFK' the key to decode it is to shift each letter back by three places. The message can then be read as 'BEWARE THE IDES OF MARCH'.

Without the knowledge of the 'key', all 25 different key combinations must be tried. This is relatively few as Caesar's is a very simple substitution cipher. A brute force attack to break it, by simply trying every possible key, would require no more than twenty-five attempts. Substitution ciphers are also susceptible to frequency analysis of the letters in the message. If the code-breaker knows what language the original message was written in then the recovery of the original message can be a straightforward matter. The most commonly used letter in English, for example, is 'e', so English language messages coded with a substitution cipher would have a different letter most commonly used. This provides good clues to code breakers.

By the 1940s, classical cryptography had become quite sophisticated. Simple substitution ciphers became more complex as 'polyalphabetic' substitutions were used. These codes used multiple substitutions controlled by a key that determines which substitution should be used for each particular letter in the original message. So, a polyalphabetic version of Caesar's Cipher could shift the first letter by one place in the alphabet, the second letter by two places, etc.

This would clearly be harder to break, but it would still be breakable. But, if the key used to determine the substitution could be generated at random then this type of cipher becomes known as a 'One Time Pad' which can be proven unbreakable, so long as the key (or 'pad') is chosen at random. On a computer system, though, it is very difficult to produce or even simulate randomness. The pad is only unbreakable if it is never reused, which implies that very large keys must be generated. Another drawback of the One Time Pad is that the keys must also be distributed to those who need to decode the messages. One Time Pads were used extensively by all sides during the Cold War with the keys being distributed via the Diplomatic Bag.

Computers can easily break many of the ciphers based on substitution. Transposition ciphers are a class of code that are much more secure than the substitution ciphers. They also rely on a key that can be used to jumble (or transpose) the letters of a message. The same key would be used to reverse the changes into clear text again. These ciphers work by rearranging the position of the characters in the original message. This avoids the problem of frequency analysis, but still provides subtle clues to an experienced code-breaker. Nonetheless, computer based transposition ciphers can provide a great deal of security.

Some ciphers employ both transposition and substitution. In the 1920s, substitution ciphers were automated in rotor machines, where a combination of wheels implements the transposition. The best known rotor machine is the German Enigma. The power of using automatic machines for code breaking was revealed when Enigma was cracked. The subsequent rise in the power and use of computers caused frequent and enormous advances in cryptography during the 1970s. In 1977, the US National Bureau of Standards set the Data Encryption Standard (DES) and in 1980 the American National Standards Institute adopted the same DES cryptographic system (technically a 'cryptographic algorithm' or 'cipher' to use the code breaker's term) for commercial use. DES is now used the world over, but recent scares about its effectiveness are causing considerable alarm.

DES is a form of private key encryption, written by IBM and adopted as a security standard by ANSI (the American Nationals Standards Institution). DES functions by encoding discrete 64 byte blocks of data up to 16 times over. (In computers one byte generally equals eight bits where a single bit represents either a '1' or a '0' of which all computer data is ultimately comprised). Each of the 16 rounds of encoding uses the same key. DES keys are 56 bits in length. A single algorithm (or cipher), standardised as 'ISO DEA-1', both encodes and decodes messages using the same private key. Security of the system is contained in the key – anyone with access to the key can access the text of the original message. Another reason for DES to be made the standard method of encryption is that the US government is able to decode any DES message using classified super-computers. In the Seventies, the US government was about the only organisation with the resources to construct such specialised, and expensive, code-breaking computers.

DES ciphers that use 56 bit keys are now in widespread use. It is used to scramble email, web browsers, pay-TV, and even the very latest electronic cash contained in so-called 'smartcards'. The bad news is that 56 bit DES can no longer be considered secure. It has been broken several times recently, and without the use of super-computers. Each year, there is a prize of $10,000 offered to anyone who can break DES – the annual RSA Laboratory's 'DES Challenge' contest. The privacy pressure group, Electronic Frontier Federation announced that it had broken DES; in July 1998, the EFF built and used the first unclassified hardware for cracking messages encoded with 56 bit DES.

The 'EFF DES Cracker', as the machine was known, took less than three days to complete the challenge, at a cost of $250,000, shattering the previous record of 39 days, which had been set by a massive network of tens of thousands of computers. The EFF also won the 1999 DES challenge as early as January, by organising thousands of volunteers who all connected to the Web and allowed their PCs to work on the problem. The EFF had effectively turned the thousands of volunteered PCs into a gigantic super-computer at very little cost using the Web.

Bearing in mind the extent to which we all use 56 bit keys in our daily life, there has been a recent worrying development in the German courts which outlines the insecurity of this technology. In Autumn 1998, a Frankfurt district court ordered a bank to repay money after a woman's bank cash card, or 'smartcard', was stolen and illegally used. The court ruled that the encryption used on the card (56 bit DES) was 'out of date and unsafe'. A German hacker, Andy Muller-Maguhn, who gave evidence in the case as an expert witness, says that the decision 'shows that customers are not sufficiently protected from criminal misuse of smartcards'. Lawyers representing the banks that support EC smartcards argued that it would be impossible for thieves to have gained access to the PIN. Their contention was that the 72 year old owner of the card must have carelessly revealed the PIN number. 'The PIN can only be cracked,' argued the bank, 'with the use of the bank's own DES key, not with the information on the card.' To crack a PIN encrypted with DES would be 'impossible,' say the banks, 'as there would be 70 billion different possibilities using the 56-bit algorithm.'

After hearing testimony from Muller-Maguhn, a member of the infamous Chaos Computer Club, the court disagreed with the banks and held them responsible for the woman's losses. The Chaos Computer Club is a long standing affiliation of German hackers that, in the past, have infiltrated many so-called secure systems all over the world. An interesting account of their activities can be found in Clifford Stoll's book 'A Cuckoo's Egg', in which he details the difficulties he had to face when trying to protect his Berkeley University computer from German hackers. The Chaos Computer Club made a statement in 1998, warning of the lack of sufficient security for smart-cards. 'Banks should take responsibility for the security holes,' the statement read, 'rather than blaming customers for negligence with the PIN or even inferring that they had criminal intentions.'

It could even be the case that some banks know that certain cryptographic products are insecure. A secret internal memo from the National Bank of New Zealand was published in 1998 by EFF Canada, which apparently acknowledges the possibility that one such product, the MONDEX electronic payment card, may be insecure. Trial versions of the card contained a microchip referred to as 3101. This microchip is known to be insecure and is regularly broken by electronics undergraduates at Delft University in the Netherlands as part of their degree course. Later versions of the smartcard which are due to go into public use, however, contain a more advanced 3109 chip.

The 3109 chip was supposed to rectify the weaknesses of the previous version. But whether the chip actually did rectify those problems was unknown and the memo warned 'the risk remains that a significant technical weakness may be found in the 3109 chips.' Naturally such a failure to meet design goals ought to render the chip useless.

However, 'this would require,' the memo continues, 'a major change to the chip which could take a significant amount of time to rectify and retest'. Not to mention a significant amount of money, but then why would a bank mention that aspect?

Rather than redesigning a new, and secure, chip for cash cards the memo suggests that the role of the possibly duff 3109 be subtly redefined. The memo suggests 'Mondex have made a general statement about the security of the card/scheme to the effect that the card is "fit for purpose". However,' observes Gavin Weekes the memo's creative author, '"purpose" is not explicitly defined in the participation agreement.' Having established grounds for a much needed way out of a potentially embarrassing problem the memo quickly offers the following suggestion: 'Statements in the participation agreement tend to indicate that the purpose is confined to "low value payments". The Australian banks appear to have a more expansive view/expectation, that the purpose covers large denomination transactions.' In other words people should be discouraged from using smartcards because they might not be safe enough. But in the meantime, go ahead. Try them out for small purchases. This is hardly the revolution for electronic trade that was promised.

EFF Canada placed a copy of the memo on its web site. Soon afterwards it also placed onto its web pages a copy of a letter from the National Bank of New Zealand which advised them to 'withdraw the Memorandum from any further display, publication, or reproduction by any means whatsoever'. EFF were also ordered to 'immediately destroy all materials that you have which contains any of the Memorandum'. Instead of complying with the Bank's orders, the EFF encouraged its supporters to 'spread this message as widely as possible, write to your congressman; and if you bank with a Mondex franchisee, move your business somewhere else!'

Many of the encryption products that are being used commercially do suffer from known insecurities, which are allowed to persist without being rectified. This is largely because of various governments' insistence that they be able to break encryption products to enable police and other agencies to engage in covert operations. A prime example of this is 56 bit DES encryption; it could be made considerably safer simply by increasing the number of bits in the key. Another version of DES uses 128 bits in the key and it is unlikely to be broken in the foreseeable future. This is not in widespread use, however, due to unfathomable US regulations that prevent 'strong encryption products' from being exported. Strong encryption is defined as cipher systems that use key lengths greater than 64 bits. US regulations governing the export of arms classify strong encryption as a munition and, as munitions, strong encryption products are subjected to strict arms control regulations. Therefore 128 bit DES, as a strong encryption product, cannot be exported since it would be classified as an international transfer of armaments.

This has led to a rather ludicrous situation. Strong encryption programs can be written with as little as three lines of computer instructions. This has persuaded one man, giving his name only as 'Cancer Omega', to have the following tattooed on to his left arm:

WARNING: THIS MAN IS CLASSIFIED AS A MUNITION [U.S. ITAR/EAR REGULATIONS -RSA IN THREE LINES OF PERL]

```
#!/bin/perlsp0777i<X+d*lMLa^*lN%0]dsXx++lMlN/dsM0<j]dsj
$/=unpack('H*',$_);$_=echo16dio\U$k"SK$/SM$n\EsN0p[lN*1
lK[d2%Sa2/d0$^lxp"|dc;s/\W//g;$_=pack('H*',/((..)*)$)
```

FEDERAL LAW PROHIBITS TRANSFER OF THIS MAN TO FOREIGNERS

The middle three lines can be typed directly into a suitably configured computer to provide strong encryption that the US government cannot break. This technically means that Mr Omega is now legally classified as a munition and he may not be exported from the US (except to Canada which is exempt from US ITAR regulations). This must play havoc with his holiday plans. It could only happen in America. Or Canada.

Within American borders, companies and individuals are free (for the time being) to produce and use strong encryption programs. Although, in the export versions of such programs the encryption must be deliberately weakened (crippled) to allow the US government to access the clear text if it desires. Netscape Corporation, the makers of 'Navigator', the most popular web browser software, felt that their overseas sales were suffering since they were unable to offer the strong encryption version of their software outside of the US. To work around the problem they took the unusual step of giving away the source code to the crippled export version of their Navigator program by allowing it to be downloaded from their web site. As soon as they released the source, cryptographers around the world set about adapting it for strong encryption. Within 22 hours of its release a strong encryption version, nicknamed 'Cryptozilla', appeared outside the US. It was perfectly legal to use as the strong encryption routines had been written outside the US.

US opposition to the spread of strong encryption is, ostensibly, for matters of national security – America needs to protect itself from terrorists, drugs dealers and the waning, albeit still present, spectre of international communism. The goings on at Menwith Hill and other stations in the ECHELON network are not merely a hang-over from the Cold War that now benefits US corporations to the tune of billions of dollars. If non-US corporations were to start using strong encryption to protect their business plans from US eavesdropping then some US companies may lose the occasional contract as the quality – and perceptiveness – of their bids drops. On the other hand those non-US companies that do opt to protect their trade secrets with strong encryption may find their access to US markets somewhat restricted, and not just by the ITAR regulations.

US industry has been opposing the restrictive, and all but useless, policy on encryption throughout the Nineties. This is largely because online trade has become possible with the advent of the Web, and in order to avoid credit card and other personal details falling into the wrong hands, encryption is vital. In response to growing demands for change, the US Commerce Department has recently relaxed export controls – but only for certain industries. William A. Reinsch, the Undersecretary for Export Administration, announced 'through the hard work of industry and government officials to finalize this regulation, US encryption firms will be better able to compete effectively with encryption manufacturers around the world'. The lifting of restrictions only applies, however, to subsidiaries of US companies.

At one stage, France also had rather draconian restrictions on encryption; displaying the computer program, noted earlier, in France carried a FF500,000 fine.

Until 1996, such encryption could only be used with the written permission of the Prime Minister. Since then, the French have implemented a system of key escrow. Key escrow is the practice of depositing private encryption keys with so-called 'trusted third parties' (TTP). The TTP will keep the key safe but will allow properly authorised government officials to access the key. In early 1999, French Prime Minister Lionel Jospin announced that the French government is relaxing its current restrictive policy on encryption. Key escrow is no longer required for domestic use of up to 128 bit encryption, and a new law to eliminate all restrictions is planned. This is similar to the policy in Finland, where there are no restrictions on strong encryption and also no legal requirement for users of such to ever divulge their encryption keys.

The breaking of 56 bit DES will inevitably lead to the adoption of 128 bit DES as a new standard for electronic commerce. It will be some time before this system can be cheaply and efficiently broken. Each extra bit in the length of the key will double the number of possible keys. If there are 70 billion possible 56 bit keys then there are 140 billion possible 57 bit keys. A 128 bit key, therefore, has an unimaginably vast number of possible keys. If the key is kept secure and distributed safely, then messages coded with 128 bit DES will be effectively unbreakable.

All the security features of the encryption methods outlined above are utterly useless if the keys needed are not distributed and kept safely. If the key is compromised, by falling into the wrong hands for example, the security of all messages that have been encrypted by the key is invalidated, and a private key must not be passed through the same channel as the coded message. Finding an alternative path for key distribution is a considerable problem – after all, if someone is spying on your email, and you wish to encrypt your mail, you cannot distribute the decryption key by email as well. It would be comparable to writing your pin number on your cash card.

Private key encryption is known technically as 'symmetric', since both parties use the same key to encode and decode messages. The problem of sharing the key is an obstacle faced by all symmetric ciphers since to be effective the key must remain private. Of course the key could be encrypted itself, but this would require another private key. That key could also be encrypted and so on and so on... The key distribution problem has been solved, however, by 'asymmetric' ciphers that use a pair of related keys, one for encoding and one for decoding. Addressing the problem of key sharing on computer based communications networks, researchers discovered the system of asymmetric key cryptography. Such systems, and there are several in use, split the key into two parts – the public part of the key and the private part. The method of asymmetric, or 'public', key cryptography is one that many people find difficult to understand. Perhaps the simplest analogy is that of a letter box, through which anyone can deposit a letter but only the person with the key to the door may collect, and hence read, the letters so delivered.

The public key is used to encode the message, and this can then only be decoded with the corresponding private part of the key. Users of such a system may safely distribute the public part of their key pairs since the public key can only be used to encode a message. The private key must remain strictly private since this is the key that will decode messages. The most important and best known asymmetric cipher is the RSA algorithm named after its inventors Ronald Rivest, Adi Shamir, and Leonard Adleman.

The RSA algorithm uses the subtle qualities of very large prime numbers to encrypt messages. RSA can in theory be broken with the standard mathematical techniques used to factor large numbers but it is not practicable to attempt to do so. The use of prime numbers means that the problem of breaking RSA is effectively equivalent to the problem of deciding if a number is prime. This is a problem that can be solved with straightforward mathematical analysis. The problem is that there are no known efficient methods to do this. With very large prime numbers (those used for RSA keys have over 100 decimal digits) it is impractical to solve the problem because it would take far too long. A typical RSA secret key would take hundreds of millions of years to crack.

Pretty Good Privacy is a strong encryption program based on RSA, written by Phil Zimmerman in the US. It is freely available for downloading on the Web and it has become the de facto standard for email encryption. The FBI is troubled by the use of PGP because it cannot read messages that are encrypted with it. Zimmerman is currently under investigation by the FBI for allegedly breaking an unspecified part of the law of the United States.

It should be noted that PGP has been used by dissidents and freedom fighters in parts of Asia to smuggle information to the West. Zimmerman says that 'In the Information Age, cryptography affects the power relationship between government and its people. PGP has become a crystal nucleus for the growth of the Crypto

Revolution, a new political movement for privacy and civil liberties in the Information Age.'

If PGP used RSA alone, the encryption process would be too slow to be useful or viable. Instead, PGP enciphers a message using a private key encryption system known as the International Data Encryption Algorithm (IDEA). The key used by IDEA is 128 bits in length giving it sufficient strength to resist any feasible attacks on the key. Each time PGP is used, a unique IDEA key is generated 'on the fly'. This so-called 'session key' is then enciphered using RSA with the public key of the person or computer that the message is intended for. In this way the message can be safely encrypted with IDEA and the weakness of key distribution is eliminated since it is exchanged separately, and safely, using RSA. This has the advantage of being both secure and fast.

An elegant – and very useful – subtlety of the RSA algorithm is that it can be used in reverse to provide another valuable service: that of authentication. In normal use, the receiver's public key is used to encrypt a message and then only the recipient's private key may decrypt it. When used in reverse a message is encrypted using the sender's private key. This means that the encrypted message can only be decrypted with the sender's public key to which anyone can safely be given access. Used in this way, RSA provides a 'digital signature' that cannot be repudiated. This is of great importance online since it allows people to prove their identities and to be accountable for what they say online.

Such a form of 'digital signature' would allow contracts to be signed online that could revolutionise international trade. It would mean that deals could be negotiated and signed via the Web with minimal cost and delay. The implications for global trade, and global efficiency, would be far-reaching as it would become much easier to shop around for the best deal at all levels of commerce. The US government is eager to stimulate trade by promoting the use of digital signatures. This does not contradict their stand on encryption because digital signatures do not conceal the content of a message. On the contrary a digital signature is used to unequivocally verify (authenticate) who produced the message. A recent trade treaty between the US and Eire was electronically signed in Dublin by Irish Premier Bertie Ahern and US President Bill Clinton, using digital signatures to demonstrate their legally binding status. Typically, however, the advantages to be gained from digital signatures were squandered by both nation's leaders who proved unable to resist the publicity and opulence of an international treaty signing ceremony.

Encryption and authentication are excellent tools for protecting one's privacy online. The Internet was, as with encryption technology, originally developed for military use. It was the product of US Department of Defense's desire for a communications network resilient enough to survive a major nuclear conflict, speculatively assuming that there would be survivors of such a war who still had something to say. The modern day success of the Web is largely a result of this ability of the Internet to reconfigure itself to utilise whatever communications resources are available. This aspect, for which it was designed, is also the feature that makes the Web such an insecure medium. Almost anybody can set up services on the Web and it can be difficult to assess trust. Without encryption and authentication the Web is no more secure, and probably less so, than speaking aloud in the street.

Now that personal computers are connected to the Internet, things have turned full circle since the days of Enigma; encryption is once again a major issue in computing. Civil liberties groups, service providers and business groups supporting online trade are lobbying in favour of encryption. They argue that legislation to restrict the use of encryption is unworkable since, as will be discussed below, use of encryption can be made undetectable. Most governments oppose unregulated use of encryption counter-claiming that it will help law-breakers evade justice. The laws being proposed around the world typically involve some form of escrow whereby law enforcement agencies may obtain a copy of anyone's secret key.

Planned legislation in the UK and elsewhere around the world is aiming to outlaw the free use of strong encryption. The government would like to retain the ability to read our email, although it reluctantly recognises our wishes to keep some things hidden from the prying eyes of the public. But nobody likes meddlers and snoops prying into their affairs – no matter who they are. What the government is suggesting is a form of key recovery facility that allows the police to access the contents of encrypted data but prevents anyone else from spying on email. All users of encryption products would be required under the proposed legislation to deposit a copy of their secret key (and any passwords) with an independent agency. The government could then obtain a court order to access key information held by the third party. This gives law enforcement agencies the ability to secretly tap the electronic communications of suspects. With very little computational cost or effort an installation such as Menwith Hill could simply add the decryption routine into its 'Dictionary' computers and continue to indiscriminately monitor email.

The key escrow legislation planned for the UK intended to cover this area, was originally proposed by Conservative cabinet minister, Ian Taylor MP in early 1997. The original public consultation document,

'Licensing Of Trusted Third Parties For The Provision Of Encryption Services', was criticised as unworkable by the IT industry and was widely opposed by the online community in Britain. The then opposition Labour Party promised that if elected to government they would abandon the proposals. The present Labour government has, however, reneged on that election promise and is now planning to introduce the scheme exactly as proposed.

Romana Machado, a civil liberties campaigner and developer of encryption products, argues that key escrow is 'the same as giving a copy of your house keys to your local police station. You'd be crazy to do that!' Of course it could be argued that in effect people do give the local police copies of the keys to their homes. These keys would take the form of police-obtained search warrants, which are often granted on the flimsiest pretexts from the courts. Police officers armed with a search warrant are authorised to use sledgehammers and other demolition tools to gain access and so do not need a physical copy of the key. Authorisation for police to enter and search particular premises is granted routinely with little or no public outcry. The suggestion that police should ever be authorised to search an encrypted file has, on the other hand, caused worldwide public outrage.

In the US there was public uproar over government proposals to regulate encryption with the so-called 'Clipper Chip'. This is a microchip that can be added to electronic communications devices to provide strong encryption in hardware. The encryption algorithm it uses is known as 'Skipjack' and is classified since it was developed by the NSA surveillance agency. It is believed that every time the chip is used the key is made available to law enforcement agencies. The Clipper Chip (along with the similar Capstone Chip) is being vociferously opposed in the US. These chips are intended to be added to devices such as mobile telephones, fax machines, and modems. Use of such devices will send all communications through the Clipper Chip that will encrypt them and thus satisfy the public demand for privacy. What has outraged Americans is that the NSA has designed Clipper so that it contains a secret 'backdoor' that allows government spies to quickly decode anything sent through Clipper.

Encryption of information is analogous to a locked door. There is little or no opposition to law enforcement agencies executing lawfully obtained search warrants so why is there such a discrepancy in attitude towards state access to encryption keys? A major concern is that, unlike searching a building, searching computerised information requires very little in the way of human resources. Computers are able to search messages automatically for suspicious behaviour, just as they do at Menwith Hill. Keyword searching is an established application of computers and there is highly sophisticated database management software on the market to assist such searching.

The cost of the computing resources required for mass surveillance of email is well within the budgets of most governments, and the additional cost of decrypting messages is minimised if the government has access to private keys. Those who oppose key escrow fear that it will make it far too easy for the governments to tap conversations as a matter of routine. Conversely, strong encryption could feasibly be used to communicate orders to terrorists or undercover espionage agents. It may also be used, of course, to encrypt illegal data files, such as stolen software, bootleg digital recordings, or obscene material, to evade detection.

But there is no reason to suppose that nefarious users of encryption would dutifully send a copy of the decryption key to the police. Why would they? Especially when there is free software available on the Web that hides the illegal use of encryption. One such program was written by Romana Machado to specifically reveal this major flaw in key escrow proposals.

Her program can hide a PGP message inside a graphic image. Modern computers can display over sixteen million colours, each of which is unique from the computer's point of view. The human eye can only distinguish around ten million different colours. Computers, therefore, can make significant changes to the colours in an image without changing the way it appears to the eye. Machado's program is a kind of electronic invisible ink that will write a message onto an image that only the computer is able to 'see'. If an encrypted message is hidden in this way it will be impossible to prove its existence without decrypting the message. The problem of law enforcement becomes even more difficult since now it cannot even be said for sure that strong encryption has even been used.

The legal status of strong encryption is in a state of flux. Attitudes to the public use of encryption range from a blanket ban (as was the case in France), to licensed use (proposed for the UK), to a complete 'hands-off' approach (as in Finland and now proposed for France). Some countries feel that any attempt to control strong encryption will fail and any laws attempting to do so will simply be ignored by law-breakers. The use of trusted third parties will make the technology less secure, and paradoxically less trustworthy, for ordinary users. It is likely, however, that an agreement will soon be reached making 128 bit DES a new international standard for electronic commerce and public communications systems. Inevitably though some countries will pursue expensive key escrow schemes. Others will rely on court orders hoping to force decryption keys out of suspects with the threat of imprisonment until the key is divulged. This is the situation in the UK at the present. A court may order a person to decode an encrypted file. Anybody refusing to do so will be held in contempt and may be imprisoned. If you're in the UK, or any country with a similar attitude, then be absolutely sure that you never forget an encryption key! Otherwise you could be sent to prison for a very long time indeed – short memories and encryption do not mix. The persistent nature of computerised information could lead to the unfortunate predicament of a person being ordered to decode a long forgotten encrypted file, discovered by suspicious police in the dusty archives of an ancient computer disk. Encryption is a powerful tool (although not quite the 'munition' that the US suggests) and should be used with care.

ASSERTING CONTROL

The chaotic state of privacy on the Web leaves users with little choice other than to take their own measures to ensure that private data stays that way. There are many services available on the Web itself, from strong encryption, total anonymity and data hiding techniques, which were discussed in the last chapter. But even the best tool is only as good as its user; if they are not properly used, they will not provide protection from prying eyes.

It is essential that personal computers are themselves kept secure. Strong encryption may keep your email private, but this is meaningless if there are unencrypted files on your hard disk containing readable copies of the email. Many applications programs will make their own copies of user data files (particularly email and web site files). These copies are often hidden from the user's view, and represents a security risk that can be easily exploited by intruders either gaining access to the machine by physically sitting at the keyboard or hacking in from the Web.

This can mean that a file the user thought was deleted from the computer is in fact still there in its pristine, original form, lurking somewhere on the hard drive. These copies can remain on the disk for months or even years, and such files can be recovered with ease by anyone with knowledge of computers. This is an inherent risk with all but the most secure computers.

The ability to delete files is essential to the operation of computers. If it were not possible to delete unwanted information, the hard disk would fill up very quickly. The structure of computer file systems is such that it makes it inefficient for the computer to actually erase the entire contents of a deleted item. When it is being used, the computer locates files by keeping an index of all of them, and this index relates the name of every file stored on the system to the part of the disk occupied by the file data. The remaining 'empty' or free space on the disk can then be calculated from this index – it will be the space that has no name attached to it. When the computer deletes a file, all it does is simply remove the file name from the index. This effectively frees the space occupied by deleted files by allowing them to be overwritten by future files.

The information contained in a deleted file is therefore not immediately removed from the computer. It remains on disk until overwritten by another file occupying the same space. It is difficult to predict when this may occur since it depends entirely upon how the individual computer is used and maintained. Ironically, this was designed as a 'safety' feature, and for good reason: most people regard the data on their computer as highly valuable and important. In many cases, it would be a disaster for such data to be lost forever as a result of hitting the 'DELETE' command by accident. The high value of information, and the ease with which it can be lost – and recovered if it has not been overwritten – has led to the development of tools that can be used to recover accidentally deleted data.

As with almost any tool, there is the potential for dual usage. As well as helping those computer users who have accidentally deleted a crucial file, or those who have had their computers damaged in some way, data recovery can be used to uncover information that people have wished to hide; it is also used for law enforcement.

There is a thriving sector of the market consisting of many profitable companies specialising in the recovery of data that has been deleted or otherwise lost. The sophisticated tools developed by such companies are able to recover the contents of almost any disk. Scott Gaidano, the president of one such data recovery company, DriveSavers, has recovered data from computer drives that have been erased, crushed, and burned. 'If we can find the hard disk, we can usually recover something,' says Gaidano. 'We've recovered files from computers that drug dealers have thrown overboard. We've even recovered files from disks that criminals try to flush down toilets. A word to the wise here: disks don't flush.'

FBI agent George Grotz says the ability to recover hard drive data is a standard law enforcement tool. 'More and more, criminals are using computers to carry out their deeds. It makes sense that we have the ability to search these machines.' And search them they do. As do Her Majesty's Customs & Excise.

Even Presidential mistress Monica Lewinsky was caught out in this way when investigators recovered 'deleted' files from Monica's seized PC. The infamous Starr Report into President Clinton's sex life cites the contents of a file on Lewinsky's computer she thought she had deleted. Investigators were able to recover the file almost effortlessly. This should serve as a warning to anyone storing private information on computer.

As already mentioned, many software applications will also leave copies of data lying around on the disk. Web browsers are again particularly bad culprits for doing this. They can improve the time it takes to display a web site by keeping a copy of it locally. By making copies of every page visited it speeds up subsequent accesses. On future visits, the browser will check whether the page has been updated since the last visit. If unchanged, it loads the copy of the page held on the disk rather than downloading it from the Web. This feature, known as 'caching', makes Web use more fluid. On the downside it effectively leaves a complete record on the disk of all the sites visited by that computer. This may be an undesirable feature for people who do not wish their family or their bosses to discover which Web sites they have visited.

The name of the cache directories can be obvious, such as 'temporary internet files', or can be hidden away deep down inside the file system. However, any software that uses a cache will have an option to turn the feature off. It may not be obvious, or easy to find, but instructions tailored for the individual browser can always be found by searching the help files that come with the browser.

Operating systems such as Windows '98 maintain their own copies of data to speed up the computer and aid in crash recovery. Frequently used data is copied to a special system area of the disk that Windows can access more quickly than normal files. This is known as a 'swap-file' since it is used to literally swap areas of memory to and from the disk. This can make the PC behave as though it has more physical memory. It also means that any data files in memory may be 'swapped out to disk' without the user knowing. Computers that are regularly backed up – as all should be – also compound the problem since copies of private files may then find their way onto back up tapes or disks.

Understanding exactly where computers store private information, and how to prevent programs from copying private files, can require considerable expertise. Most popular software fails to assist those who require privacy and wish to disable these features. The default configuration of web browsers and operating systems allows the programs to copy files without asking. To ensure that data remains private these features should be turned off. This is not as easy as it sounds.

As already emphasised, the commands to disable this behaviour are often hidden away in obscure menus disguised behind esoteric, and usually system-dependant, naming conventions. Reading manuals and requesting technical support is advisable, but not always helpful. Possibly the best source of help and advice on specific

Internet software problems is the Web itself. Often by simply typing your question into a search engine, dozens, if not hundreds of pages will be available describing exactly what needs to be done.

Looking at how intelligence agencies deal with keeping digital data truly secret can shed some light on the problem. Computer security experts often wryly advise that any data that must be kept secret should not be entered into a computer at all. This isn't surprising since many top-secret orders have been handed down by word of mouth. If secret data really must be entered into a computer then, to ensure it remains secret, the machine must never be connected to any other device. Both the US and British military operate a policy of isolating sensitive computers. Any CIA computer storing secret data is never attached to publicly accessible networks. In British military establishments, all sensitive computers must be kept in locked rooms from which even the presence of a telephone line is disallowed.

The dangers of networking computers or attaching them to the telephone system are well understood. The dangerous nature of hard disks is only recently coming to light. It was initially thought that unwanted data could be erased from hard disks by simply overwriting the disk space that contained it. Unfortunately, it is not that simple. Data recovery experts, and probably intelligence agencies before them, discovered methods to analyse the magnetic structure of the disk surface to recover data overwritten in the normal way. The implication of this is that once data has been placed onto a computer it can become very, very difficult to erase. Computer data is therefore surprisingly persistent and remain in existence long after a person thought it deleted. This problem is in the nature of the storage media itself and is difficult to avoid.

The surface of a hard drive is similar to video and audiocassettes, which are magnetic tapes. Information is recorded on them as a magnetic pattern. The heads that read and write data to and from such magnetic media can only detect magnetic forces that are above a certain minimum strength. Devices that are sensitive to smaller levels of magnetism are sometimes able to recover overwritten data by filtering out the strong signal of the new data and analysing the weak signal in the background. This is similar in effect to listening to a whisper in a room where people are shouting. Computer equipment is particularly adept at filtering out the shouting and amplifying the whispers.

Recovering data in this way is an expensive process that requires specialist equipment, and only large corporations reliant on high-value data and the espionage community can afford such services. It was thought that overwriting the sensitive data many times would make it impossible for it to be recovered, even with the most sophisticated equipment. So-called 'secure' erase software became available that would actually attempt to drown out all traces of deleted data by writing a cryptographic pattern over the area.

The cryptographic pattern is as close to randomness as is possible on a computer system and the idea is that it will effectively mask any overwritten data from being recovered – since investigators would, in theory, need to know the cryptogram used to 'wipe' the disk.

The evidential value of recovered data to spies and law enforcement has fuelled the development of ever more sophisticated, and expensive, equipment to recover data erased in this way. So, removing data from a computer system is no easy task. Paul Baccus, a technical engineer with an Oxfordshire based data-recovery firm, describes an extreme method of data-erasure: when GCHQ decom-

mission old computers, they adopt a unique and somewhat extreme practice to ensure that no data can ever be
recovered from discarded disks.

Armed police escort unwanted GCHQ tapes and hard
disks from GCHQ directly to the nuclear power station at
Sellafield. There, they are dipped into the nuclear reactor,
where the high levels of radiation permanently destroys
the data. It also renders the remains of the disk highly
radioactive further discouraging any attempt to recover
residual data.

The facility to nuke unwanted data files out of existence is not available to all but a select group, and nor is
it ever likely to be (would we want to do it even if we
could?) The best advice possible is to encrypt all private
data as a matter of routine. That way, if the encrypted file
is recovered, then it cannot be read. But, this might not
be safe enough. A list of Web resources, including strong
encryption, is included at the back of this book.

A computing establishment of the Royal Air Force,
which for legal reasons cannot be named, once asked a
Cambridgeshire data recovery firm to restore the data
from an RAF hard disk that had been accidentally
damaged. The RAF officer told the firm that the data on
the disk had been encrypted so the recovery experts
should not expect to find readable data on the disk. The
encryption technique used by the RAF to protect their
secrets worked by scrambling the location of its files on
disk and distributing the contents of files across the entire
surface of the disk in a seemingly random pattern.

Unfortunately for the RAF this is precisely the way in
which computer disks normally operate. Even worse was
the news that the data recovery techniques used will
automatically attempt to unscramble damaged disks. The
data recovery firm contacted the RAF to inform them that
not only had they recovered the lost RAF data but an

unavoidable side effect of the process had resulted in all the 'encrypted' files being decoded as well.

The cryptographer who had devised the RAF coding system simply did not understand how computer files are stored on disk and hence he produced a system that was desperately ineffective. This is a problem for all encryption systems – it is impossible to know if they are truly secure. Any strong encryption program could be broken, and thus rendered useless, tomorrow.

Truly secure computer systems have encryption technology built into them from the ground up. On these systems all data is encrypted as soon as it enters the computer. Unencrypted data would never be stored on disk. Home and office computers do not provide such a facility and, if the lawmakers have their way, they never will. If they do, they would not be truly safe because a less secure system would be prescribed.

The issues outlined above are only the issues of privacy that exists on standalone computers. Portable and laptop machines are particularly vulnerable as they are more likely to be stolen. However, when computers are connected to networks, their security is reduced even further.

Email privacy is best secured by using strong encryption. Programs such as PGP (Pretty Good Privacy) provide unprecedented levels of security and are easy to use. It is unlikely, although not impossible, that PGP could be broken.

PGP can also provide strong encryption for files stored on hard disks and it has the facility to perform 'secure' deletion of files by overwriting them with a cryptographic pattern. Files deleted in this way could only be recovered with expensive specialised equipment. It is also possible to prove your identity on the Web by using PGP to attach a digital signature to your messages that prevents anyone from modifying or forging your name.

Browsing the Web is another online activity that can and should be made more secure. Sharing data with a secure site on the Web can usually be considered safe – and even safer when using a browser such as 'Crytpozilla' that has strong encryption enabled. Sending credit card details and other sensitive information to such sites is safe. The problem isn't so much what happens to your data whilst it is 'in flight' but what happens to it once it arrives at its destination.

Can you really be sure that your privacy will be respected by the organisation you are dealing with? This is a particularly relevant question when dealing with sites that have no legal requirement to do so, such as those in the US. If a site is not to be trusted then it should be treated with care.

All Web addresses in the world are registered with the Internet Network Information Centre (INTERNIC), which is responsible for allocating names to web sites. INTERNIC maintains its own site which includes a search facility that allows anyone to verify the name and address of the providers of all commercial participants.

There are several methods of browsing web sites with a degree of anonymity. The simplest is to use a 'proxy server'. This is a machine that sits between a web browser and a web site. Browsers send instructions to the proxy about which pages they wish to download from the Web and it is the proxy that will go off and fetch them. This means that all the web sites visited through a proxy may only log the address of the proxy server and will not be able to ascertain who is the ultimate visitor.

Larger networks such as service providers, universities, and corporations usually operate proxy servers. There is, however, a growing number of publicly accessible proxy servers that may be used by anyone. ISPs advise their users on how to access the their proxy. The details of using public proxy servers are not always given but there are several web sites dedicated to listing all of them, complete with the configuration details needed to use them.

The proxy is able to keep a log of every page visited. This could pose a potential problem for ensuring privacy, and one has to judge whether the proxy can be trusted with such knowledge.

Recently, adaptations of the proxy server make it possible for a small fee to make web browsing sessions anonymous. These will keep no logs and will remove any information that could allow the 'anonymised' machine to be traced. Again, it is a matter of how willing the user is to trust such a service.

Anonymous email has been available on the Web for years. One of the earliest anonymous email services was based in Finland, and it allowed anyone to both send and receive email with apparent privacy. Anonymous email is used by millions of people for safe discussion of sensitive issues. Campaigners for democracy also use it to report human rights violations from around the world that may otherwise have gone unreported.

Some of the reasons for using anonymous email are given by privacy expert and author André Bacard. 'Maybe you're a computer engineer who wants to express opinions about computer products, opinions that your employer might hold against you. Possibly you live in a community that is violently intolerant of your social, political, or religious views. Perhaps you're seeking employment via the Internet and you don't want to jeopardise your present job. Possibly you want to place personal ads. Perchance you're a whistle-blower afraid of retaliation. Conceivably you feel that, if you criticise your government, Big Brother will monitor you.'

Anonymous email may not be quite as anonymous as it purports to be. The Finnish penet email service was closed down after it was allegedly used to criticise the actions of the Church of Scientology. Penet was founded in 1992 by Johan Helsingius and it handled around seven thousand messages a day serving over 200,000 users. The service had an excellent reputation for trustworthiness partly due to Finland's good record on individual rights, privacy, and freedom of speech.

In February of 1995, however, Helsingius was informed by the Church of Scientology that his email service was being used to put private Church of Scientology documents on the Web. They had reported this as a theft to the FBI. They demanded that Helsingius reveal the identity of the person who had posted the information to the Web.

Helsingius refused to reveal the identity of users of his anonymous service and the next day, the FBI informed him that they had received a request from Interpol to obtain the name of the anonymous poster and they would obtain a search and seizure warrant if necessary. A few days later, the Swedish newspaper Dagens Nyheter published an article claiming that the penet service was being used to anonymously post child pornography to the Web. The article, based on investigations by Mats Wiklund of the University of Stockholm, was quickly followed up by scare stories in the Finnish press about the Web being 'flooded', according to one newspaper, 'with child porn'.

In fact, Helsingius financed the anonymous service out of his own funds and due to its popularity he had to limit the maximum size of any email messages it sent. Sending images via email results in large file sizes that were automatically rejected by the penet system.

Wiklund's 'research' into alleged abuse of anonymous mail contained little hard evidence and the only picture he referred people to seems to have been a photograph of a naturists' camp. Of the five thousand pictures studied by Wiklund, only eight contained adolescents and none of these could be described as pornographic. Helsingius undertook to track down the pictures that had caused concern, and discovered that they had in fact been posted from the United Kingdom by a person who had forged an email address so that it looked as if it had been posted from Helsingius' system. It is quite easy to forge an email address, but also a simple matter to detect forgeries.

Some writers on the Web suggested without any hard evidence that there was a connection between Wiklund, the person forging the penet address, and Church of Scientology's attempts to close down anonymous email servers.

Most such uncorroborated accusations came, however, from anonymous sources. Finnish police served a search and seizure warrant and raided Helsingius, taking away his computer systems. Speaking about the raid Helsingius says 'I am pretty shocked! The police have gotten a search and seizure warrant on my home and gotten the real email address of a user that has allegedly posted material stolen from the Church of Scientology.'

The user involved was based at the California Institute of Technology (Caltech). Shortly after the search and seizure in Finland, the Caltech security office was approached by private investigators who wanted to know the true identity of the of the holder of the email account discovered by Finnish police. Caltech refused to give out any information on its users and later the same day an attorney representing the Church of Scientology, Helena Kobrin, also demanded the information. Kobrin was referred to the General Counsel's office and the name of the email user continued to be withheld.

The Computer Crime Unit of the Los Angeles Police Department (LAPD) then contacted Caltech requesting more information on the case. They had received a report that the owner of a certain email address at Caltech had broken into Church of Scientology computers and stolen documents that were then posted 'anonymously' to the Web from a Caltech computer system. Caltech co-operated with the police, giving them the name of the user in question on the understanding that the police would not reveal it to any third parties. The LAPD later informed Caltech that no evidence of a crime had been found.

The private investigators and Kobrin persisted in the efforts to obtain copies of the email sent by the person they were investigating. Kobrin even produced a letter allegedly signed by the account holder granting the Church of Scientology permission to access the data. After noticing irregularities with the letter, Caltech security made a quick telephone call to the account holder and permission for the Scientologists to access the data was again denied.

The Director of the Caltech Campus Computing Organisation feels that the entire affair was simply an internal row with the Church of Scientology. He says 'Our analysis is that Caltech was caught in the middle of what appears to be an internal matter between the Church of Scientology and one of its members, who also happened to be an account holder on the Caltech alumni computer. No evidence that a Caltech computer was used to break into another computer, or was used to store stolen documents could ever be found.'

A second attack on the penet system was carried out by the Church of Scientology in 1996. This time they were demanding the names of two further anonymous users. After Helsingius was again ordered by the Finnish courts to give up the information, the British newspaper The

Net Spies

Observer ran an article on Helsingius in which they claimed he was facilitating the distribution of child pornography on the Web. Shortly afterwards Helsingius closed the penet anonymous server.

There are many other anonymous email servers available on the Web but these no longer support the ability for people to receive email anonymously. They can only be used to send anonymous messages.

Presumably these services keep no logs of the people that have used them, making them effectively untraceable. Of course, they could be logging everything but this is a matter of trust between the user and the service provider.

A word of warning on so-called anonymous mailers: foreign and domestic intelligence agencies are actively monitoring worldwide Internet traffic and are running anonymous re-mailer services. Defence experts Paul Strassmann (the former US Assistant Secretary of Defense) and William Marlow say that anonymous re-mailers pose an, 'unprecedented national security threat from information terrorists. Intelligence services have set up their own re-mailers in order to collect data on potential spies, criminals, and terrorists.' Despite this many people are still prepared to continue trusting such so-called secure email services.

Financial privacy in online transactions is another area that can be easily improved, not by technology but by an understanding of what the actual risks are. In a survey of Internet users carried out by USA Today and IntelliQuest, it was found that only 5 per cent of users would send their credit card details across the Internet. This is in contrast to 77 per cent who trust automatic teller machines – the 'hole in the wall'. To overcome this perceived weakness of online commerce, most banks and credit companies are supporting the use of strong encryption.

When credit card details are sent over the Web it is technically possible for them to be intercepted by an eavesdropper. If the transaction is performed with weak or no encryption the card number could, feasibly, be stolen. Users perceive this as the greatest threat to their financial security and yet there have never been any reported incidents of credit card details being stolen in this way.

Indeed, security experts at Reuters challenged a competent hacker to do just this. The hacker was able to do so within a few hours but he told the security that he could have obtained the same details much more quickly by simply hacking into one of the machines, rather than listening in to their communications.

There have been many reported incidents of credit card details being stolen from the Web in other ways. Some of these incidents have involved the theft of files containing hundreds of thousands of credit card numbers. All of the incidents have one thing in common, though, and that is that they have been stolen from hacked computers and not by eavesdropping. Credit card provider VISA has been spending millions on a publicity campaign to emphasis that Web transactions are at least as safe as any other use of credit cards. Indeed, Web transactions that use strong encryption are probably the safest way of using a credit card. The Vice-President of Visa Electronic Commerce, Joseph Vause, regards Web based credit card transactions as 'nearly invulnerable'.

'As far as we know,' says Vause, 'there has been no in-flight credit card data stolen. This makes on-line credit card use safer than "in person" transactions. In a restaurant, you hand your card to a waiter and they walk away with it for a while. Online, no one's looking at your card when you're sending it to the merchant.' Most of the credit card numbers that have been stolen from computer networks belong to individuals that have never even used the Web. They have made a purchase in the normal way, by telephone or over the counter, and the firm they have been dealing with has subsequently entered their details onto insecure computer systems.

But once the credit card details have been entered onto a firm's online computers, it becomes vulnerable to theft. In 1997, Carlos Elipe Salgado was arrested at San Francisco International Airport for attempting to sell 100,000 credit card numbers to undercover FBI agents. Those numbers were stolen from various commercial computers attached to the Web. Salgado pleaded guilty to charges of hacking and fraud and was sentenced to 30 months in prison. The infamous hacker Kevin Mitnick is also accused, among other things, of stealing 20,000 credit card numbers in one hit from a commercial computer. Mitnick was awaiting trial in Los Angeles as this book went to press.

Companies attaching their insecure systems to the Web is the real thing to worry about. In December 1998, a confidential conference of Internet industry analysts, sponsored by IBM's Global Services division addressed this issue. At the meeting, IBM officials disclosed that they maintain a team of 'ethical hackers' who successfully break into ninety percent of computers used by online stores to hold credit card data. Cal Slemp, IBM's Global Offering Executive for Security Services, confirmed the percentage but declined to name which stores were the target of the faux break-ins. 'We are successful over 90 per cent of the time,' Slemp said.

Commenting on the worrying statistic a spokesman for the US Federal Trade Commission exclaimed: 'Yikes! I don't think we know about that around here.' This is a very worrying statistic since almost every use of a credit card, both on and off the Web, will eventually end up on a computer somewhere. Hackers are then often able to use the Web to access those and other private records of consumers.

Vause says the VISA monitors online commerce sites, and it will pull card accounts from those sites with excessive 'charge backs', or customer refunds, due to fraud. 'We've done it in the past, and we'll continue to do it in the future,' he said. Federal regulators in the US say that consumer protection laws buffer the effects of credit card theft for online shoppers. 'I don't think that (the IBM study) should deter consumers from shopping on the Web,' says Federal Trade Commission Director David Medine. 'The use of credit cards is still the best method for shopping, online or off. But,' he says 'the IBM statistics should serve as a wake-up call for sites to be much more careful.'

Companies that are storing private data on individuals should take more care to protect themselves from hacking and those that fail to do so should be named. Consumers need to be given the choice to trade with organisations that can guarantee their privacy. In the EU companies are now legally required to provide such protection and will be held liable for any losses incurred if they fail to comply. In the US and other places, however, there is no requirement for companies to provide such protection. The answer is obvious for people who wish to protect the privacy of their transactions: don't trade with countries that will not protect your privacy.

The Web itself is an ideal place to find help in protecting privacy. Organisations such as Privacy International, the Electronic Frontier Federation, and Network Associates (the distributors of PGP) maintain extensive Web sites that contain much useful advice and software for protecting online privacy. Virus checking software can be useful to prevent hostile programs such as Back Orifice from breaching computer security. Highly sensitive data such as private keys and passwords should not be stored on computers that are ever likely to be attached to the Web. They should only be entered directly as and when needed.

Software enhancements, such as the feature of Microsoft Windows that allows the computer to remember passwords should be disabled. Many of the features of web browsers, such as caching and JavaScript, should also be disabled. Unfortunately many of the features that need to be turned off to maintain privacy are the very features that make the Web easy to use. There is always going to be a trade-off between privacy and ease of use until such a time that computer manufacturers and Web service providers are legally required to protect the privacy of their customers. This is unlikely to happen in the near future and in the meantime it is up to the individual to discover what security risks exist on the web sites they visit.

THE FUTURE

Online privacy issues are not going to go away. While this book was being researched, many privacy-related stories hit the headlines. Diverse issues caught public attention from the French government's abrupt change of policy on encryption, to the Irish school-girl whom, it is claimed, has devised a method breaking RSA encryption.

As this book was going to press, Intel, which manufactures 80% of the processors used in desktop computers, launched their Pentium III amid a storm of protest from privacy rights groups. Each Pentium III is electronically 'tagged' with a unique serial number, which the processor can use when communicating with the outside world. A prime example of this is when the computer visits web sites that wish to identify visitors. According to Intel, the processor ID number would enable web users to conduct secure online transactions, as according to Intel, the site could verify one's identity by querying the processor's ID.

However, the Web is designed to be open, but this openness means that people can access and use the Web from any available machine, be it their home or office PC, a PC in an Internet Café, or a public access terminal in a library. The point is that people are not tied to a single place of access, and hence the processor ID is an inadequate proof of identity for the roaming user. Several of Intel's trading partners were also present at the launch of the Pentium III launch ceremony held in San Jose in California's Silicon Valley. David Pedigo of The Sabre Group said that processor IDs were, 'a valuable tool for corporate asset-tracking and authenticating users in business transactions. Passwords can be compromised, and mechanisms such as cookies and digital certificates can be copied or accidentally erased from a hard disk. But the chip serial number is an indelible part of the chip, and – when used in conjunction with other authentication mechanisms – can provide a reliable mechanism for ensuring a user is who he or she claims to be.' This is of course based on the assumption that user sticks to using just the one computer and does not upgrade his or her processor.

Notwithstanding these potential problems, The Sabre Group's director of applied technology, Andrew Abate, quite naturally agreed with his colleague. 'Passwords and cookies can be burned', he said. 'We have contracts with travel agents in good faith, and we have agreements with foreign governments by treaty requiring us to charge tariffs on transactions. These contracts and treaties require a reliable authentication mechanism to determine who The Sabre Group is doing business with.'The Sabre Group went on to demonstrate a prototype of a 'secure' program for travel agencies that can read the processor ID to determine who is using a particular system before dispatching information customised for that user. Are they assuming that processors are used only by one person?

Another of Intel's partners, Computer Associates, demonstrated an asset management program. This could read the processor ID across a network and allow a company to keep track of the whereabouts of its computing assets. 'The processor ID determines what applications and operating system should be on each PC', said Computer Associates' David J.P. Corriveau, the Senior Vice President of research and development. This sparked another privacy fear since it suggests that the processor ID could be linked to software licensing information.Privacy advocates are mainly concerned by the risk that processor ID could be used to track users of the Web and their activities. Each time someone provides personal information to a commercial web site, that information could be linked to their processor ID. It is conceivable, and also highly likely, that companies could share such data and build up vast databases on individuals based on their processor ID.

Online privacy groups joined forces to fight the massive Intel organisation, calling for a boycott of Pentium III chips under the banner 'Big Brother Inside' – playing on Pentium's marketing campaign, 'Intel Inside'. The fear among privacy advocates is that processor IDs will make online anonymity impossible. This is a view shared by reporter Scott Rosenberg who says that, 'Intel set out to design a scheme to defeat the anonymity that people take for granted on the Net – without ever asking consumers whether they wanted it or liked it or would design it differently themselves.'

Opposition to the processor ID has been widespread and Intel were forced to advise manufacturers of PCs to turn the ID feature off. By default, the processor ID is enabled during the manufacturing process. It is up to the PC makers to run special software to disable the ID function. The consumer may then, in theory, choose whether or not they want their processor to identify them to any site on the Web that asks.

However, C'T magazine, based in Germany, reports that it is possible for the ID function to be secretly turned on or off by web sites without the user's knowledge or consent. Responding to Intel's claim that this feature would give the user control, Christian Persson, Chief Editor of C'T, says, 'We have proven this is wrong.' According to Persson, Intel in Germany has confirmed that the ID number can be reset in this way.

Speaking from Intel's headquarters in Santa Clara, California, spokesperson Tom Waldrop says, 'The way we designed it was to make it difficult for someone hacking or sending a virus over the Internet to reset the serial number without your knowledge.' He acknowledges that it is difficult, perhaps, but not impossible; 'It is conceivable that a control utility can be hacked or a serial number read, but it's very difficult.' Waldrop revealed more when he posed questions himself, 'You have to ask – what would be done with the number after it was read? What good is it to anyone anyway?' Indeed, but then it could be argued that if it isn't any good to anyone anyway, as Intel spokesman Waldrop claims, then why on earth did they bother building it into the processor in the first place?

The Electronic Privacy Information Center (EPIC), one of the organisers of the 'Big Brother Inside' campaign, named after Intel's campaign, 'Pentium Inside', are demanding that Intel recall all Pentium III chips and permanently disable the ID feature. 'It looks like a pretty serious flaw,' said EPIC policy director Dave Banisar. 'It's been one disaster after another for Intel. It was inevitable that someone would discover how to do something like this. All of Intel's claims that people's privacy was going to be protected was built on a house of sand.'

Persson, however, does not think that the processor ID is a serious invasion of privacy. He points out that most hardware has a serial number, including all hard disks, which theoretically could also be read over the Web. 'This is not such a big issue,' he says. 'I do not understand all the fuss. I think people do not like Intel so much and use this to kick their ass.' Maybe that is so, but the favourite target for this kind of 'ass kicking' has to be the huge, and sometimes maligned, Microsoft Corporation.

Microsoft has also been the target of a recent privacy controversy because of their software registration scheme. Software piracy (or 'bootlegging') is rife both on and off the Internet since digital data is so easy to copy. Microsoft, along with other software providers, feels as though it is not making profits as high as it perhaps should. The Microsoft registration scheme requires legitimate owners of Microsoft products to obtain a code from Microsoft that will enable their software. This code is tied to the individual configuration of each user's PC. This means that Microsoft will be able to link individual users with individual machines on the Web, and so it is just another way in which data profiles may be amassed on individuals. The scheme is currently on trial outside the US.

Inside the US, the need to identify web users is also driven by the Child Online Protection Act (COPA). This law requires the operators of web sites that contain adult oriented material to verify that visitors are over the age of 18. Web sites that fail to comply face a $50,000 per day fine and the operators face up to six months imprisonment.

COPA is regarded by many as a completely unworkable law and is currently being challenged in federal court by the American Civil Liberties Organisation. So far the only method being used for age verification on US adult web sites is to take a credit card number – and we all know the risks that entails.

Besides the unnecessary risk of giving out your credit card number, it also assumes that children are unable to type in credit card numbers. This is particularly foolish as there are lists of credit card numbers available on the Web, which will always pass validity checks. If this seems a little beyond the grasp of your average teenager, consider the fact that there have been instances of teenagers hacking into the FBI and cash point machines from their bedrooms, and schoolchildren who have allegedly cracked fiendishly difficult encryption codes.

'Intel and Microsoft both want to know who you are; so, too do the Feds,' says Salon magazine's Scott Rosenberg. Junkbusters Corp., and the Electronic Privacy

Information Center say that, 'experience shows that consumers will be coerced into submitting to the tracking mechanism.' Internet access providers such as America On Line and Compuserve are among the fastest growing companies listed on the stock exchange. Could this be because they are in the enviable position of knowing exactly what their customers are doing on the Web whilst also being in possession of their names and addresses? It is a worrying trend that huge American corporations are compiling massive databanks on individuals free from any legal responsibility to take care of that data.

Another worrying trend is in the steps that are being taken to control the public use of encryption. The UK and US governments among others oppose the use of encryption and are trying to ensure that they will be able to decode all encrypted data. The UK's proposals for licensing trusted third parties (TTPs) is, as we have seen, being vigorously opposed. Electronic market traders, however, are keen to exploit the Web and they wish to offer potential customers the illusion of security. Banks are supporting them, and there are plans afoot to launch a so-called 'secure' scheme for online trade.

This scheme will involve digital certificates and encryption methods agreed upon by both banks and the traders. This will allow customers' identities to be verified through digital signatures, and the verification process will be performed by independent organisations. Because of this, the scheme will be marketed as secure – or trustworthy. But in effect, this scheme is precisely the same as the licensed TTP scheme proposed by government and opposed by almost everybody else. There would be no licensing with this scheme and take-up of both the scheme and the encryption it relies on would be purely voluntary.

One has to wonder what will become of those organisations that refuse to voluntarily enter the scheme. Will they be forced to the sidelines of the market? The scheme will be offered to consumers as a revolutionary new form of electronic trade, when in reality it is simply a means of bringing in TTPs by the backdoor. It is regulation of encryption by stealth.

Personal information is the ultimate asset in Web-based trade. Some companies and individuals will go to any lengths to obtain personal information. So much so that many people are fighting back by actively 'polluting' online databases. When one is not making a personal gain there is no legal requirement, in most countries, to give out true information. Many people are attempting to reduce the market value of consumer databases by seeding it with false information.

Also, people campaigning against the ECHELON Dictionary computers will add likely keywords to every message they send in a bid to overwhelm the system. They will add words such as 'gun bomb drugs kill the president' to ensure that all of their email is flagged by the Dictionary as suspicious and requires a human to make a decision.

Many sites ask for an email address claiming that they will keep it private, and not disclose it to any other organisation. Some people will deliberately create a new email address just for the web site, and not allow anyone else to know that address. Any junk mail that subsequently arrives at that address must surely invalidate the company's claim to be protecting private data.

The argument that privacy is unnecessary if you have nothing to hide is often put forward, but it is a weak argument. Such an argument relies on a one-way relationship of trust – that of the individual trusting business and the authorities. It also implies that people cannot be trusted to behave themselves – give them the right to privacy and they will automatically indulge themselves in unspeakable acts. The government (and the world of commerce), so the argument goes, can be trusted not to abuse our basic privacy. Since there is plenty of evidence to contradict this assumption, it can be safely said that most people would rather retain the option of privacy.

Automated surveillance computers are growing in number and usage, and the notion of privacy as a right is diminishing. The Web will undoubtedly dominate communications in the next century, and it is an ideal medium for automatic mass surveillance. It threatens to provide the State with unprecedented powers to monitor, and hence control the population. Computer-based surveillance is a growth area, and its products are growing more and more sophisticated. Far from being a tool for empowerment, the Web is threatening to become a pervasive observer. Silently watching, recording, and analysing the population, it will dutifully alert its shadowy masters to those individuals that it considers to be 'of interest'.

Both the Web and encryption were originally military tools, and they are still widely used in the defence sector. Military hardware has always been monopolised by governments. History teaches us that control of military hardware is essential to maintain a hold on power. This control nearly came to a globally suicidal conclusion when the ranked masses of intercontinental ballistic missiles were aimed and ready to fire during the Cold War. We are now facing the unknown consequences of 'infowar' – a term used by military planners and strategists, describing a situation where an aggressive enemy turns the nation's reliance on computer technology against them. In such a war, it is control of software that is of far more importance than hardware.

The Internet and strong encryption are two pieces of

military software that have found their way into the public domain. The tools available to hackers have clear military applications, and one wonders if anonymous enthusiasts can write programs such as Back Orifice, just what software tools are available to hostile nations and terrorists? It may not be quite as simple as uploading a virus onto enemy computers, as depicted in the film 'Independence Day', but the principle of information warfare is valid. A hostile power that gains control of its enemies' computer networks could wreak havoc. In such a conflict, military hardware could just as easily be turned upon its owners as fired on the enemy – reminiscent of James Bond's heroic re-targeting of the Spectre missiles that destroyed the insane Blofeld in 'The Spy Who Loved Me'.

Today's society is almost totally reliant on computer systems, and the prospect of 'info-war' is no longer as far fetched as it once seemed. The 1980s film, 'Wargames' depicted a narrowly averted nuclear conflict, which was triggered by a teenage hacker who had infiltrated weapons computers. Modern military research is not aimed at infiltrating enemy weapon control computers, as these are likely to be isolated and physically protected. Instead, methods are being developed to attack enemy weapon communications computers in the command and control (C2) structure. The aim is not so much to destroy enemy data, but to confuse the enemy by modifying the data on such computers. Commandos of the future that go behind enemy lines will need to know how to hack into computers and install false data into the enemy's C2.

A major hacking attack is a real fear of Western defence analysts. In the US in the late 1980s, there was a strong belief that such an attack was imminent, either by a foreign power or by subversives. When the AT&T telephone network crashed in 1990, millions of Americans were deprived of a telephone service. The crash, which caused the loss of millions of dollars worth of trade, was initially thought to be an attack by hackers. The high level of American government paranoia surrounding hacking actually led to the arrest of a New York hacker Mark Abene as a suspect. The Secret Service seized Abene's computer equipment, presumably to perform a detailed search of the information on his hard disks. No evidence was found to link Abene to the AT&T crash and shortly afterwards AT&T admitted that the crash was caused by a basic programming error in their equipment. The incident gave the US government a fright, however, and it launched a crackdown on computer related crime.

The 'Hacker Crackdown' as it became known, led to long terms of imprisonment for many hackers and a continuing succession of unworkable legislation. These were the first mass arrests under the Computer Fraud and Abuse Act and the Electronic Communications and Privacy Act (both passed in 1986). The crackdown was aimed mainly at preventing theft and to protect the telephone system from wilful damage. It was seen by many as a Draconian clamp down on personal freedom denying people free speech over public data networks.

The Electronic Freedom Foundation (EFF) operates one of the most popular Web sites in the world and its 'Free Speech Online', symbolised by a blue ribbon, is featured on millions of web sites across the world. The EFF describes themselves as a non-profit civil liberties organisation working in the public interest to protect privacy, free expression, and access to public resources and information online, as well as to promote responsibility in new media.

The issue of privacy is currently centred on cryptography, and in particular on strong encryption and public key methods. The EFF promotes the use of cryptography for electronic mail, equating it to the use of an envelope in the surface mail.

The EFF was founded after the Steve Jackson Games case. In March 1990 the American Secret Service mounted a widely publicised and ultimately disastrous operation when it attempted to close down Jackson's publishing business.

The Secret Service claimed that a Jackson employee had links to the hacker underworld. They seized a computer bulletin board containing private email belonging to hundreds of innocent people and also seized a manuscript that they considered to be 'a handbook for computer crime'. In fact, the document was simply an outline proposal for a computer game.

The futility of the seizure is emphasised when one considers that information on bomb making, and the manufacture of illegal drugs is widely available on the Web both inside and outside of the jurisdiction of the US Secret Service. Much of information seized by the Secret Service is also freely available. People began to see the tremendous threat posed to civil liberties by the Secret Service and this, along with some other well-publicised operations, led to the formation of the Electronic Frontier Foundation – whose initial purpose was to fight such violations of freedom.

Steve Jackson won a lawsuit against the Secret Service who were chastised by a Federal Judge for their actions and were ordered to pay $50,000 damages to Jackson along with $250,000 legal costs. The mainstream press, however, carried little publicity of this important event.

We have moved on somewhat from the hacking fears that beset the authorities in the late 80s and early 90s. Since then, the Internet has been transformed from an academic 'plaything' into a mass market service. Commercial organisations are now eager to exploit this new marketplace in both the sphere of sales and market research. No one is opposing plans to make online sales easier for the consumer, except when it implies a loss of online privacy.

Privacy invasions involving hidden webcams (web cameras) are another threat but what is being done to prevent this? Sadly, little can be realistically done to prevent someone hiding a camera and broadcasting it over the Web. It unfortunately remains up to the individuals who have had their rights violated to discover broadcasts, and seek redress under whatever means that exist in their local territory, if indeed there is an such machinery.

In 1995, in Alaska a high school janitor had been video-taping young girls while they were changing in the locker room. But, because of the absence of laws governing hidden cameras, he could only be prosecuted for trespassing. In the same year in New Orleans, Steven Glover installed a video camera in the attic above his neighbour's bed. He could not be prosecuted because there was no law against doing this; Glover could only be tried for obtaining illegal entry. The prosecutor in the case, Jerry Jones, was aghast, saying: 'If I'm a Peeping Tom and I look into your bedroom, I can be prosecuted. If I put a video camera to do the same thing and I do not record sound, I am committing no crime.' Recording of sound would change the nature of the crime into 'oral interception' which, unlike videotaping, is covered by anti-bugging legislation. It is possible that videotapes obtained in such a way and broadcast over the Web could contravene obscenity laws but, as Jones points out, to prosecute for this would currently involve having to play the tapes in court, which would only cause further embarrassment to the victims. The victim in the Glover case, who wishes to be called 'Melissa' says that Glover's lawyers, 'tried very hard to intimidate me, saying the videos could be shown in the open courtroom.' There is also the possibility that once such a tape is put on the Web, multiple copies could be made and placed everywhere, as with the Anderson-Lee video. There would be nothing the courts could do to recover and destroy all such copies.

This is the nature of computer information. It is persistent, unlike printed information that can be withdrawn and eventually forgotten. Once anything is entered onto a computer, and in particular onto computers that may become attached to the Web, that information can remain in existence forever. It may be inaccurate, illegally obtained, or embarrassing, and it may return years later to haunt the victim.

The shocking lack of proper privacy safeguards on the Web threatens everyone; not just the 'wired' users online. Only international agreements on the protection of privacy can stem the growing tide of 'dataveillance', but such an agreement is not forthcoming. The European Union and the United States are openly talking about the possibility of a future data trade war as their respective stance on privacy becomes increasingly incompatible.

So what does the future hold? The prospect for online privacy, and privacy in general is looking bleak. Our rights are being eroded, and unless we take active steps to preserve the rights that people have fought for, often paying with their lives, we stand to lose our right to privacy – both online and in everyday life. The Internet is ungoverned – and some would say ungovernable – and at present, it is not subject to international laws. It can therefore be used for good or bad. The only solution available is self-regulation combined with a strong code of personal ethics; the exercising of one's rights while having respect for others' rights. This responsibility must ultimately rest with each and every user of the Internet.

Net Spies

USEFUL RESOURCES AND
RECOMMENDED READING

WEB SITES

The following web addresses were correct at the time of going to press. Neither the publisher nor the author endorse the contents of these sites, nor take any responsibility for the accuracy of their contents.

THE INTERNIC

http://www.internic.net/

This site provides information on the registered owners of Internet domains. A domain on the Internet is any address of the form www.some.where. All domains have to be registered at InterNIC to prevent two or more web sites from using the same name. Every registered domain is stored on the InterNIC's 'whois' database. This database can be accessed freely from the InterNIC's web site and provides the name and contact details of the owner and administrator of every commercial site on the Web. It does not provide information about individual users of the Web – just the people who own and operate web servers.

ELECTRONIC FRONTIER FOUNDATION

http://www.eff.org/

A non-profit organisation dedicated to promoting privacy and freedom on the Web. EFF run many campaigns and their web site is constantly updated with current events online. They also provide a searchable database of past issues of rights and freedom online. The EFF home page is ranked as one of the most popular sites on the Web.

ELECTRONIC PRIVACY INFORMATION CENTRE

http://www.epic.org/

EPIC is a public interest research centre based in Washington, DC. It was established in 1994 to focus public attention on emerging civil liberties issues and to protect privacy. EPIC have brought many cases to court. The EPIC web site contains many useful resources including an online bookstore, an archive of formerly secret documents obtained under the Freedom of Information Act, and guidebooks on how to use much of the freely available privacy enhancing software.

EUROPEAN UNION INFORMATION

http://www.europa.eu.int/

The official repository of all online information of the European Parliament and Commission.

UNITED KINGDOM GOVERNMENT INFORMATION

http://www.open.gov.uk/

The main starting page for the British government's Open Government initiative. It can be used to find abundant legal and official information on British law and policy.

Useful Resources and Recommended Reading

UNITED STATES GOVERNMENT

http://www.whitehouse.gov/

The homepage of the White House is an amusing launch pad to access most other web sites run by the American government.

US NATIONAL SECURITY AGENCY

http://www.nsa.gov/

The official home page of the ultra-secret American spying agency. It provides many documents on security and cryptography. It is unlikely to give out on information on the ECHELON Dictionary system that the NSA operates.

THE NET SPIES OFFICIAL WEBSITE!

http://www.net-spies.co.uk/

The home page of this book! Please visit.

PGP HOME PAGES

http://www.pgp.com/

From this site, operated by Network Associates International, it is possible to download the popular PGP encryption program. It also contains advice on public key encryption, news from Phil Zimmerman (the writer of PGP), and a directory service for finding email user's public keys.

RSA (ENCRYPTION INFORMATION)

http://www.rsa.com/

RSA is a well known provider of encryption products and services. Their web pages provide lots of useful information on the technology of, and emerging issues in cryptography.

PHRACK

http://www.phrack.com/

Phrack Magazine covers many security issues from the perspective of the hacking community.

CERT

http://www.cert.org/

The Computer Emergency Response Team is a state funded team of computer security experts that study Internet security vulnerabilities. CERT regularly publish the latest details of security related incidents to allow systems administrators and user to maintain tight security of their computers.

2600

http://www.2600.com/

A hacker's group dealing with the legal implications of hacking and detailing many of the more serious incidents of the past decade. They provide much information on computer security issues and the activities of government agencies online and the manner in which the treat (or mistreat) suspects. There are also links to many interesting sites.

BACK ORIFICE

http://www.cultdeadcow.com/

The official site of the writers of Back Orifice. The Cult of the Dead Cow are in many ways a useful resource for security and privacy information online although their presentation is unorthodox to say the least. Not for minors.

INTERNET SEARCH ENGINES

These are only a few of many popular search engines:

http://www.yahoo.com/
http://www.altavista.com/
http://www.excite.com/
http://www.lycos.com/
http://www.infoseek.com/
http://www.webcrawler.com/

BOOKS

THE CUCKOO'S EGG
Tracking a Spy Through a Maze of Computer Espionage
Clifford Stoll
(Pocket Books)

TAKEDOWN
The Pursuit and Capture of Kevin Mitnick, America's Most
Wanted Computer Outlaw – By the Man Who Did It.
Tsutomu Shimomura, John Markoff
(Warner Books)

THE CODEBREAKERS
The Comprehensive History of Secret Communication
from Ancient Times to the Internet
David Kahn
(Scribner)

THE HACKER CRACKDOWN
Law and Disorder on the Electronic Frontier
Bruce Sterling
(Bantam)

THE OFFICIAL PGP USER'S GUIDE
Philip R. Zimmermann
(MIT Press)

GLOSSARY

ALGORITHM
A mathematical term that describes a procedure for solving a problem by breaking the problem down into a list of simple steps. Computer programs are all algorithms since they all consist of long lists of repetitive but simple instructions.

BIT
The smallest possible representation of data on a computer. A bit can be either a '1' or a '0'.

BYTE
A unit of computerised data. A byte usually contains eight bits, and often stores a single character of text.

CAPSTONE
See Clipper

CIPHER
An individual encryption technique, such as the Data Encryption Standard, is known as a cipher. See 'Encryption'.

CLIPPER
Clipper and Capstone are proposed microchips that would be able to decode any messages encrypted by American communications products. These microchips were designed by the ultra-secret US National Security Agency and they are both widely and vociferously opposed as a violation of civil rights.

CRYPTOGRAPHY/CRYPTOLOGY
The practice of encoding message. See Encryption.

DES (DATA ENCRYPTION STANDARD)

The official system for encoding electronic data in the US. DES is in worldwide use by commercial organisations. In its present form DES is considered by many privacy advocates as unsafe.

DATA IMPERATIVE

A label given by the press to the rush for corporations and governments to acquire as much personal information on individuals as possible. The Data Imperative has been fuelled by the high commercial value of such databases.

DPA (DATA PROTECTION ACT)

The United Kingdom law concerning databases. This Act was recently updated to bring it in line with European Union regulations. In its present form the DPA places strict responsibilities on the owners of computerised data and it provides redress for members of the public.

DOWNLOAD

The act of copying a file from the Web. When a user takes any information from the Web onto his or her own computer they are downloading.

EFF ELECTRONIC FRONTIER FOUNDATION

A non-profit making organisation that promotes freedom, privacy, and ethical behaviour online. For more information see the EFF web site – address to be found in the list of resources.

ENCRYPTION
This is the generic term for techniques that disguise a written message by converting the words into a secret code. Individual methods of encryption are called ciphers.

ENIGMA MACHINE
This was the coding device used by the German High Command to communicate with troops in the field during World War II. Enigma was broken by a team of British researchers at Bletchley Park who, as part of their research, developed the world's first computers.

HACKING
The process of 'breaking in' to a computer system after accessing it via a network connection. Programmers sometimes use the term to describe the process of fixing a difficult or obscure computer program that is not working. In some countries hacking is now regarded as a criminal offence.

IDEA (INTERNATIONAL DATA ENCRYPTION ALGORITHM)
IDEA is a strong encryption technique in widespread use on the Internet.

IP ADDRESS
IP stands for the Internet Protocol that forms the heart of the Internet. Every machine on the Internet has to have a unique IP address in dotted decimal form. For example, 204.253.162.4 is the IP address of the Electronic Frontier Foundation's Web server.

KEY ESCROW

This is a system that would enable government agencies to access the contents of encrypted messages. All encryption techniques rely upon some form of a secret key to 'unlock' the coded message. Escrow of the key simply means giving a copy of it to the government before one is permitted to use encryption.

KEYWORD SEARCH

This is a powerful technique for analysing computerised text documents. The search program (or search engine) is provided with a list of words and it can then search through possibly millions of documents, marking for attention all those that contain the given words or phrases. Keyword searches are in widespread use for many different applications. Keyword searches cannot be used on images.

LAN (LOCAL AREA NETWORK)

A local area network is the smallest kind of computer network. There are wide area networks (WAN), metropolitan area networks (MAN), and the Internet. The Internet is the system that can connect all of these different networks into one, seamless, network. In fact most of the networks attached to the Internet are local. LANs are operated by companies, government departments, and educational establishments.

MAIL BOMBING

A 'mailbomb' is an attempt to deprive an individual or organisation of their email facilities. Mailbombs can be delivered in one of two forms, either a very, very large file which will hog the resources of the computer it is sent to, or as thousands of identical copies of the same message.

The result of both methods is the same: email on the 'bombed' machine becomes unusable.

PHONE PHREAKING
A term from the early Seventies craze of hacking the telephone system. Phreakers were able to use international trunk lines to bypass the billing equipment in the telephone system. In this way they could make telephone calls all over the world for free. The vast majority of phreakers were not thieves but simply hobbyists dedicated to discovering what this system was capable of. It is interesting to note that some of the early phreakers have risen to become some of the biggest and most influential names in the computer industry.

PGP (PRETTY GOOD PRIVACY)
PGP is a program used to encrypt computer data files. Written by Phil Zimmerman and originally based on the strong RSA algorithm, PGP has become the de-facto standard for email encryption. It is downloadable from the Web for free.

RSA ALGORITHM
This is a powerful encryption technique named after its inventors Rivest, Shamir, and Adleman. RSA solves many problems of online encryption and it formed the basis of early releases of the PGP program.

SEARCH ENGINE
A web page that can be used to find the addresses of other web pages that contain items of interest. Internet search engines use 'keyword searches' on vast databases of web pages and generates for the user a list of sites that contain the words searched for. The most popular search engines on the Web include Alta Vista, Yahoo! and Excite.

SMARTCARDS

So-called 'smartcards' are rapidly replacing the present form of swipe cards. Instead of a magnetic strip smartcards have an embedded microchip that holds data such as the card number, the cardholder's name, and in some cases the amount of 'electronic cash' stored on the card. Within the next few years all existing credit and cash cards will be replaced by smartcards.

SOURCE CODE

All computer programs are written as text files. The text consists of a list of instructions to the computer in a form that is close to both spoken language and mathematics. Source code is convenient for the programmer to read but difficult for a computer to interpret. Hence most programs are 'compiled' from the source code into a form more suitable for computer programs. It is very difficult for a human to interpret compiled programs so to protect the copyright of source code this is how most programs are distributed.

SPAM

Junk email. See UCE.

SYSTEM ADMINISTRATOR

All multi-user computer systems, such as those operated by Internet Service Providers, have an administrator, usually just called a 'sysadmin' or 'sysop'. The sysadmin's job is to ensure that the computer is operational, and available at all times. The sysadmin is also responsible for security and as such will have access to the contents of every file on the machine(s) he or she is responsible for.

TCP (TRANSPORT CONTROL PROTOCOL)

This is the system that allows messages to be delivered from one computer on the Web to another. It complements IP to form the TCP/IP suite, which is in effect the Internet itself.

UCE (UNSOLICITED COMMERCIAL EMAIL)

Often referred to as 'spam', UCE is the electronic equivalent of junk mail. Thousands of junk email messages are sent every day. It is regarded as a major problem for email users since it is very easy to collate vast mailing lists containing millions of email addresses, which can then be bombarded with junk messages.

WEB BROWSER

Software packages such as Netscape Navigator, Microsoft Internet Explorer, or Hot Java (among others) that is used to access and view web pages. Although by no means the only method of accessing the Web such browser software is, for many users, the standard. The rapid growth of the Web in recent years was driven largely by the free availability of web browser software.

WEB CACHE

A web cache is a directory on a user's own computer that stores copies of all pages that the user has recently been looking at. Sophisticated web browsers all use a cache by default since it can speed up access to frequently visited pages by loading them from the user's own disk drive if the browser detects that the requested page is unchanged since the last time it was viewed. Some browsers refer to the web cache as 'temporary internet files'.

WEB SERVER
Large commercial machines that form web sites. The web server machines are permanently available computer systems that can be viewed from anywhere by web browsers.

INDEX

Other titles by Vision Paperbacks

I Spy
The Black Art of Bugging
Dr Frank Barnaby

Information is power, and spying has become highly profitable. The latest gadgets make it possible to eavesdrop on any rival, whether for love or greed. Dr Barnaby is a leading expert on surveillance and he focuses on the illicit use of bugging devices for private gain. He shows how easy and cost-effective the bugging business has become; how industrial espionage is a vibrant profession and how the biggest companies are the most unscrupulous 'private spies' of all. Rivals are not the only ones to be targeted; a firm's own employees may be spied upon if they step out of line.
I-SPY exposes this world of intrigue and immorality through the testimonial of those that do teh dirty work, those who employ them and their victims.

£9.99
ISBN: 1-901250-14-8

The Mind Controllers
Dr Armen Victorian

Politics is said to be all about the battle for men's minds, and so is spying. The intelligence community has conducted an enormous variety of questionable experiments in an attempt to control the way people think and act. More than 10,000 former 'guinea pigs' in over 20 countries say they were exploited, and harmed, without their consent. They include hospital patients, pregnant women, school children, prisoners and veterans.

THE MIND CONTROLLERS examines the Pentagon's experiments with psychic techniques following the discovery that Russia was researching parapsychology for covert missions. Millions of dollars were spent on extrasensory perception, remote viewing, LSD, telepathy and brainwashing.

Using the US Freedom of Information Act, Dr Armen Victorian has assembled documentary proof of these programmes. Avoiding conspiracy theory, his book is the first to explore in depth, the murky and secretive world of mind control.

£9.99
ISBN: 1-901250-26-1

Who Killed Diana?
by Peter Hounam and Derek McAdam

The fatal car crash that claimed the lives of Diana, Princess of Wales, Dodi Fayed and their driver, Henri Paul, shocked the world on August 31 1997. But was it simply a horrific accident, caused by the driver being drunk, or were there more sinister forces at play? Countless investigations have appeared in the wake of the accident, pointing to many puzzling aspects of the disaster, but none have shed light on the growing and wodespread suspicion of a murder plot.

In WHO KILLED DIANA? as award-winning former Sunday Times journalist reveals hard evidence that a sinister plan to kill the coule was hatched two weeks before they died, sensationally challenging the official view.

£9.99
ISBN: 1-901250-17-2

The Hemp Handbook
Gisela Schreiber

The dried leaves of the hemp plant produce the 'soft drug' known as marijuana, cannabis, pot or hashish. As such, it is banned in most of the world arepartaking is supposedly dangerous. This book aims to demythologise hemp and its by-products. As a healing substance, it has been used for millennia by many civilisations including the Greeks, Romans and Egyptians. The Hemp Handbook is therefore an essential source of information for those engaging in the great current debate - whether marijuana should be legalised.
It points out that as a raw material, and renewable resource, hemp can be used in the manufacture of paper, insulation, clothes and rope. As medicine, it helps glaucoma, cancer and AIDS sufferers. And as a recreational drug, its use is now unstoppable. The author, a medical journalist based in Germany argues for a radical rethink.

£9.99
ISBN: 1-901250-28-8